T0194960

A FOLLOWER of CHRIST

Five Identifying Characteristics

ROBERT BALL

WESTBOW
PRESS®
A DIVISION OF THOMAS NELSON
& ZONDERVAN

WestBow Press books may be ordered through booksellers or by contacting:

WestBow Press
A Division of Thomas Nelson & Zondervan
1663 Liberty Drive
Bloomington, IN 47403
www.westbowpress.com
1 (866) 928-1240

Scripture taken from the King James Version of the Bible.

ISBN: 978-1-9736-8198-4 (sc)
ISBN: 978-1-9736-8200-4 (hc)
ISBN: 978-1-9736-8199-1 (e)

Library of Congress Control Number: 2019920625

Print information available on the last page.

WestBow Press rev. date: 12/10/2019

Contents

Introduction

In the eighth and ninth centuries AD, a man named Charlemagne united most of Europe under one organized Christian government. Through military conquest, Charlemagne subdued both the Lombards and the Saxons. During the thirty years of Charlemagne's conquests and expanding government, Christianity was spread to every conquered region of Europe. Thousands—hundreds of thousands—professed publicly to Christian conversion and were baptized. Some have touted this period of history as particularly relevant in the expansion of the Christian faith along with considerable expansion of Christian learning among all of Europe. However, one might ask, how exactly was such a noteworthy evangelistic effort carried out? How exactly did so many people profess faith in Christ and become Christians—followers of Christ? History reveals that Charlemagne's evangelistic efforts were dubious at best. It seems that conquered peoples were forced to become Christians on pain of death. In other words, if a conquered person refused to renounce his or her pagan beliefs and embrace Christianity with a public profession and baptism, that person was executed. The Saxons were particularly resistant to Christian conversion. History records the terrible atrocities brought upon the Saxons for refusing to be Christianized by way of baptism.[1] Thousands of Saxons were put to the sword for refusal to be baptized and thus be called Christians. Charlemagne's methods certainly produced high conversion numbers, which no doubt the church of his day reveled in; however, the true effect of such practices was devastating and patently unbiblical. It would be safe to say that most of those forced conversions

---

[1] Philip Schaff and David Schley Schaff, *History of the Christian Church*. (New York: Charles Scribner's Sons, 1910), 103.

were no conversions at all. Multitudes agreed to be baptized and take the title of Christian to save their lives. Charlemagne produced many Christians by title; however, very few were genuinely redeemed by personal saving faith in Jesus Christ. Many were counted as followers of Christ, but very few knew Him or really followed Him.

While I am thankful that, for the most part, there are no systems of forced Christian conversion in the twenty-first century, I am concerned we are making the same mistake, nonetheless. As a pastor, I am often engaged in outreach ministries, prayerfully seeking opportunities to share the gospel with those who need the good news of God's saving grace. The ministry affords many opportunities to interact with professing Christians and non-Christians alike. I have noticed over the last twenty years a certain proliferation of the term "follower of Christ." It seems more and more people claim to be followers of Christ, and yet the evidence often reveals a complete lack of understanding as to what it means to be a follower of Christ. I do not make that statement from a mean-spirited or legalistic position; it is simply an honest observation as the result of evangelistic interaction with various people on an almost daily basis. For example, there are times when I am engaged in a conversation with someone, and as soon as I mention God, Jesus, or the fact that I am a pastor, the person almost stumbles over himself or herself to tell me he or she is a Christian. It seems that somehow the word *Christian* is deemed a magic phrase that is supposed to stop me short of sharing the gospel with that person or, heaven forbid, keep me from saying anything about sin and our need of a Savior. Rather than joyfully engaging in a conversation about our mutual Savior, I am summarily dismissed as if the person said all the right things, and I should go away.

Unfortunately, the biblical idea of being a Christian seems to have been supplanted by a contemporary form that is kinder, gentler, and more socially acceptable. Furthermore, it almost seems religiously chic, in certain social circles, to claim the title of Christian. Society appears ready to accept Christianity, but only on its terms and only when the religious mood suits the occasion. One might even go so far as to say the idea of claiming to be a Christian brings a certain feeling of security. Rather than deny God completely, the lost world is content with taking the title, hoping for the salvific benefits, while rejecting the literal biblical call to a surrendered life and repentance from sin that is part and parcel to true saving faith in Christ.

With regard to being a biblical follower of Christ, this book is neither groundbreaking nor earth shattering. My motive is simple—to clearly articulate the biblical principles and doctrines that pertain to being a follower of Christ. To call oneself a follower of Christ does not necessarily make it so. God has clearly set forth how we must come to Him and how we become genuine followers of His Beloved Son. In the early church, the first followers of Jesus were called Christians because of their noble dedication to a life of obedience to Him. The first century Christians were saved by faith, and they walked by faith before a lost world that clearly noticed the difference. By contrast, many twenty-first century Christians walk among a lost world, and no one notices. I would suggest many contemporary Christians look so much like the world in lifestyle and demeanor that no one even cares that they call themselves Christians.

So what does it mean to be a follower of Christ? I would suggest there are some distinct elements in the life of a true believer that identify that person as a follower of Christ. I believe there are five distinct elements we can draw from the Bible that help define what it means to be a follower of Christ. First, being a follower of Christ involves a relationship with Him. This seems to be the simplest, perhaps most obvious element of being a follower of Christ, however, I fear it is the one element most often overlooked. It is easy to profess Christianity. There are multitudes of churches to choose from, and if you enjoy the experience of the worship service, you're in. The truth, however, is that no one has ever been saved by association. No one has ever been saved because he or she had an emotional experience in the presence of Christians. The only thing religious exercise can do is give a person a false sense of security. The Bible is crystal clear that the only way to be a genuine follower of Christ is to have a saving relationship with Him. That relationship comes by way of confession of sin and saving faith in Jesus. Unless a person has been saved by faith in Jesus, that person is not saved at all. If a person has never been saved by faith in Jesus, he or she is not a follower of Jesus.

I recently spoke with a woman who told me she was raised Baptist. Clearly, she did not understand that a religious denomination has nothing to do with being saved. She then went on to tell me she just could not get up on Sunday morning to attend the local church service; Sunday is her day off, and she wanted to sleep in. She further expressed her desire to let her children decide for themselves if they wanted to attend church or not. She was quick to tell me she was a Christian, but none of the things she said aligned with what the Bible tells us concerning a person who has a saving relationship with Jesus. It is impossible to follow Jesus from afar. It is impossible to be a genuine follower of Christ in the home and that example fail to have a profound impact on our children. This woman was a follower of Christ in name only.

The second element of being a follower of Christ involves what I call apprenticeship. When we talk about apprenticeship, we most often think of professional training under the tutelage of a master craftsman. For example, a person who is learning to be an electrician may work under the supervision and direction of a master electrician. By working alongside the master electrician, the apprentice learns the requisite skills of the trade. A genuine follower of Christ has entered a lifetime of spiritual apprenticeship. We call this the process of sanctification. The redeemed child of God lives daily under the tutelage of God the Holy Spirit. The Bible is our textbook, and the world is our classroom. We not only learn from the Holy Spirit; we also learn from association and fellowship with other Christians. Being a true follower of Jesus involves life-long training and learning. Those who claim to be followers of Jesus and demonstrate no evidence of learning from the Master are failing in their responsibility as a genuine follower of Christ. A person who has no interest in learning to emulate our Savior is most likely living out the fact that they have no saving relationship with Him.

The third distinct element of being a genuine follower of Christ involves spiritual growth. Spiritual growth is very similar to physical growth. Just as we must eat the right foods and exercise our bodies to grow and be healthy physically, so the spiritual man must feed on the right food and be exercised in the law of God. Just as a baby begins life consuming milk and then moves up to the meat and potatoes, spiritual babes in Christ must start out on the milk of the Word and eventually move on to the meat of the Word. Spiritual growth is essential for one who would be a genuine follower of Christ.

Fourth, being a follower of Christ involves effectiveness in the Christian life. It is a contradiction of terms to claim followership of Christ and yet make no contribution to His kingdom work or to the accomplishment of the things He has called us to do. Those who are genuine followers of Christ will be involved in the work Jesus has set before us. If a person claims to be an automobile mechanic, and I never see him work on cars, I might begin to doubt his claim to be a mechanic. As my wife has pointed out from time to time, a mechanic shop that has the same cars sitting out front all the time lends evidence that the mechanic there is not very good. Likewise, if a person claims to be a follower of Christ, and he or she is never engaged in the affairs of Jesus, one might rightly begin to question the genuineness of the person's claim. The evidence of a genuine followership of Christ can be seen in the applied and effective Christian life.

Finally, being a follower of Christ involves courage. The world is steadily becoming more and more antagonistic toward those who love and serve God. If we profess to be a follower of Christ and align our lives with His Word, the world will resist our message and, in many instances, resist us personally. If we live for Christ in this life, there will be a price to pay. It may be as simple as being ostracized from a group, or it may be as painful as suffering personal attacks. The redeemed of Christ are called to the front line in the realm of spiritual warfare. It takes courage to serve our Lord in this world.

I pray the unfolding of these five elements in the following pages will be a blessing and encouragement to you in your Christian walk. Perhaps the information in this book will be an opportunity for you to take inventory in your own life. Perhaps the information in this book will be an opportunity for you to be sure you are a genuine follower of Christ. I pray you are.

One

RELATIONSHIP

S everal years ago, I was blessed with the opportunity to meet a young church-planting pastor who was planning a new church in the community where I pastor. The church model he proposed and employed presents a concert-style worship service in an ultracontemporary setting with a high-energy message. The lights are off in the congregation throughout the service, while spotlights illuminate the stage, the singers, and the pastor as he speaks. Every part of the service is choreographed and carried off in impressive fashion. The church has grown, and the attendance at its weekly services is impressive. This young church planter came to town with a plan to attract people to his new church, and he has certainly been successful in drawing the crowds.

Among all the things the pastor shared with me that day was one statement that caught my attention and played over and over in my mind. He said his goal was to invite people to be followers of Christ. He wanted to get them in the building so he could invite them to follow Jesus. On the surface, that statement sounds good. After all, who would be opposed to inviting others to be followers of Christ?

However, upon deeper reflection, I realize that calling people to be followers of Christ without telling them how to be followers of Christ is to invite spiritual disaster. If we imply that following Jesus means coming to a church service, enjoying the concert, hearing a life-lessons message, and then going home until next week, we have seriously misled them! There is the danger that we might create a false sense of security because the people think they are followers of Christ by association with a church. How tragic it would be for such a person to die and then hear Jesus say,

"Depart from me for I never knew you" (Matt. 25:41). As ambassadors of Christ in this world, we must be sure the gospel message we share majors on a new spiritual birth and relationship with God the Father through faith in Jesus Christ.

Where to Begin

No matter the liturgy (the form of public worship) a church may employ, whether it be full-on contemporary, high church chanting, or anything in between, the gospel message is required if we expect a lost person to come to Jesus in saving faith. The apostle Paul said, "For I am not ashamed of the gospel of Christ: for it is the power of God unto salvation to everyone that believeth; to the Jew first, and also to the Greek" (Rom. 1:16). The gospel is the power of God unto salvation—not worship music, not emotion, not atmosphere, not feelings, not religious affiliation, and certainly not a new or unique church model. The idea behind the word *power* in this verse is transformation power. The message of the gospel has the power to transform a person's life. A person who hears the gospel is made aware of his or her lost condition in sin and thus drawn to place faith in Jesus unto forgiveness and salvation. At the moment of saving faith, the lost person is born again spiritually and transformed from being spiritually dead to being spiritually alive. A truly saved person will never be the same again. Nothing but the gospel has that kind of transforming power.

Knowing this to be true, contemporary church has begun to employ an amazing number of methods to get people to attend church. The stated purpose is to get the lost people in the building so we can share the gospel with them. However, the method soon subverts the gospel and becomes the dominant reason people attend church—not the gospel and certainly not the clear presentation of the Word of God. For example, I recently drove past a church that was raffling off a car! This church invited people to attend its services so they could buy a raffle ticket and perhaps win a new car. This church seemed to kill two birds with one stone. It raised money and drew a large crowd of people. I saw another church pay for food vendor trucks to sit in the parking lot so people could buy food as they came in and out of church. Another church had the Easter bunny greet all the children as they came to church on Easter morning. There are a lot of ways to entice people to come to church, but the Easter bunny at the door takes the cake for me. The fact is that whatever method a church might use to get people in the door—and some of those methods are dubious at best—it will be the method that must continue to be employed to get them to come back. Unless the gospel of Jesus Christ is presented—the power of God unto salvation—all the methods in the world will not produce followers of Christ. The people will simply attend for the new car, the food truck, or even the Easter bunny.

If we desire to make followers of Christ, we must begin with the message God begins with. When we read the Bible, we discover that the gospel message begins with our sin. Our sin problem finds its origin all the way back in the garden of Eden. God created the first human being—Adam. Man did not evolve from a lower life-form, a pool of water with some protein in it, or some accidental combination of ingredients. The theory of evolution is scientifically untenable and mathematically impossible. Man was created by God, in the image of God, to have fellowship with Him and serve Him forever.

Because Adam was created in the image of God, he was a moral agent, just as we are today. That means Adam had the ability to recognize right from wrong. As a moral agent, Adam had the responsibility to choose right and abstain from wrong. What was true of Adam was true of Eve as well. They were both created in the image of God as moral agents, and they were both responsible before God to do right and abstain from wrong.

Adam and Eve started life in moral perfection. They were created morally perfect; they had no sin. Their sinless perfection allowed them to enjoy unhindered fellowship with God. They could converse with God, ask Him questions, learn from what He taught them, and in general enjoy His magnificent presence. Adam and Eve experienced what it was like to live in perfect peace, contentment, joy, and love. They had a perfect relationship as husband and wife while enjoying perfect fellowship with the God who created them and blessed them with the garden of Eden.

Then God gave Adam and Eve a test. They could enjoy the fruit of every tree of the garden except one. God said, "Of every tree of the garden thou mayest freely eat: But of the tree of the knowledge of good and evil, thou shalt not eat of it: for in the day that thou eatest thereof thou shalt surely die" (Gen. 2:16–17). The test was incredibly simple. God gave Adam and Eve an abundance of fruit trees in the garden of Eden, all of which they were completely free to eat of as they desired. There was, however, one tree God said was off-limits. The tree of the knowledge of good and evil was forbidden; they were not to eat of it. The test was simple. Would Adam and Eve obey God, or would they disobey God concerning the one forbidden tree? As free moral agents, they had to choose. As free moral agents, they would be personally responsible for the consequences of the choice they made. God even went so far as to tell them the consequence for disobedience. He told them that in the day they ate of the forbidden tree, they would certainly die. The penalty was death.

The test was then enhanced by the introduction of Satan. The sacred writer introduced Satan as the serpent. "Now the serpent was more subtil than any beast of the field which the Lord God had made" (Gen. 3:1). The word *subtil* means shrewd, cunning, or clever. The subtle nature of Satan means he is crafty and not to be trusted under any circumstance.[2] Satan easily took advantage of Eve's innocence. Neither Adam nor Eve knew anything about evil—not even the potential of evil. Satan had the advantage when the dialogue began. Satan was and still is the master of evil and rebellion against God. Satan convinced Eve to doubt God's command and His goodness. Eve chose to disobey God; she ate of the forbidden fruit. Adam came along and rather than rebuke his wife, he partook of the same fruit and thus the same sin. Adam and Eve were given a choice: believe God and live or reject God's Word and die. They chose to disobey God, and the penalty was death.

The path of sin and disobedience that Adam and Eve walked is the same one we walk today when we choose to disobey God. The Bible tells us, "And when the woman saw that the tree was good for food, and that it was pleasant to the eyes, and a tree to be desired to make one wise, she took of the fruit thereof, and did eat, and gave also unto her husband with her; and he did eat" (Gen. 3:6). The three areas of temptation Eve experienced and succumbed to are the same three areas of temptation we experience in life every day. Eve saw that the tree was good for food. This is what we call the lust of the flesh. There are many things in life we think will be good for us, but there is one problem; God said no. He said it is not good for us.

---

[2] Kenneth A. Mathews, *The New American Commentary: Genesis 1–11:26*, vol. 1A, (Nashville TN: Broadman & Holman, 1996), 232.

The boundaries God sets in our lives are for our own good. God knows what is good for us far better than we know what is good for ourselves.

Then Eve noticed that the fruit was pleasant to look at; we call this the lust of the eyes. We can associate with this element of temptation as well. There are many things in life we might look at that will initiate a sinful desire in our heart. Perhaps we look at our neighbor's house, and jealousy sets in because we want a house like he has. Maybe we see someone in a new car and suddenly we are not thankful for the car God gave us. Then there are the sins of the eye that have to do with lust and immorality. Satan has so orchestrated this world that we are bombarded with immorality on every side.

Finally, Eve saw that the fruit was desirable to make one wise. This is known as the pride of life. It is here that Eve began to doubt God's goodness. Perhaps Eve began to reason that God was holding out on them. She might have thought, *I want to eat this fruit and be like God.* There are many temptations in life today that seem to be wise, but they are nothing more than seeking to live life outside of God's sovereign design. We always get into trouble when we allow pride and selfish desires to rule our thinking and decision making.

Eve was the first person to succumb to Satan's enticement. However, the proverbial nail in man's moral coffin took place when Adam decided to follow his wife in disobeying God. Adam's sin was the one that infected the entire human race. Adam was created first and therefore was the representative of all humanity. It was Adam that God had charged with caring for the garden of Eden. It was Adam to whom God delivered the prohibition concerning the forbidden tree. It was Adam's responsibility to share God's instruction with his wife and then to watch over her. While it is reasonable to presume Adam would not have been standing next to Eve every moment of the day, we cannot help but ask: Where was he when Satan was deceiving his wife? Furthermore, we might reasonably expect a different reaction from Adam once he realized what his wife had done. Rather than respond with any form of horror or shock, Adam willingly joined in the sin. Rather than rebuke her for disobeying God, Adam allowed her to lead him into the same sinful choice.

Because of Adam's sin, every human being born after Adam is born with a sin nature. Every human being born after Adam comes into this world as a sinner from birth. Adam passed his sin nature to all of humanity. The apostle Paul said it this way: "Wherefore, as by one man sin entered into the world, and death by sin; and so death passed upon all men, for that all have sinned" (Rom. 5:12). Because we have Adam's sin nature, we commit acts of sin. For example, we tell lies because we have a sin nature that moves us to do so. We lust after what is not ours because we have a sin nature that moves us to do so. The sin we commit begins in our own hearts and then is manifested in our lifestyles. A sinful lifestyle is simply the outward expression of a heart problem—an inherent sin nature.

Because sin is every person's most serious spiritual problem, that is where we must begin when we want to bring a lost person to Jesus. There is no benefit in bringing a lost person into a church service and making him or her feel comfortable. There is no benefit in bringing a lost person into a church service and entertaining that person. There is no benefit in bringing a lost person into a church service and making the individual feel like part of the club. Unless we talk about sin and what it means to be lost in sin, the lost person will never know that he or she is lost. We must start where Jesus started; we must deal with the sin problem.

I recently had the opportunity to talk with a young man who is sixteen years old. He ran into some trouble with local law enforcement and was assigned some community service hours to be served. We routinely allow young people to do their community service at our church. Part of the requirement to do community service at our church is a meeting with me or one of the other staff pastors. As I began to talk to this young man about his situation, I asked him about his relationship with Jesus and if he knew what it means to be saved. His response was straight to the point. He said, "I don't know what that is." This young man had no idea what it means to be saved. I asked him if he knew what sin is. I then asked him if he is a sinner. He admitted he is a sinner, which then opened the way for me to tell him of the consequences of sin. I told him that he is spiritually dead in his sin and separated from the God who created him and loves him. I then had the great privilege to share with him how to be forgiven of his sin by saving faith in Jesus Christ. The young man was not ready to pray and receive Jesus at that time, but he promised to read some literature I gave him and to let me know if he changed his mind. The point of the story is this: we might do any number of things to get this young man in the door of our church. However, unless we confront him with the gospel, he will never be genuinely saved. It would be a travesty to have this young man attend our church services every week and then die and go to hell. We must deal with sin if we hope to make a difference in a person's life.

Coming to Grips

Introducing a person to the concept of sin and our inherent sin guilt before God is only part of what we need to share. One of the most difficult things for our contemporary society to come to grips with is the fact that we cannot save ourselves. Secular humanism has created a culture of self-reliance. There is a pervasive belief that man can overcome his weaknesses and flaws. Secular humanism believes that man is the ultimate authority and that all our problems and failures can be solved or cured through education and science. This philosophical paradigm has influenced society's view of sin and how to solve it. Christianity is often viewed as just one of many religious practices whereby a person can clean up his or her moral life and become a better person. The idea that humans somehow control their own destinies regarding sin is fully expressed in the false idea that if people somehow do more good than bad in their lives, they will be rewarded with entrance into heaven. The Bible clearly tells us that's not how it works. No one has the inherent ability to save himself or herself from sin. There is absolutely nothing we can do to solve our sin problem. Our sin carries a debt we cannot pay. No amount of good works, acts of penitence, religious sacrifices, or personal effort can restore us to a right relationship with God. The prophet Isaiah said our best effort at righteousness is no better than filthy rags before God (Isa. 64:6). We cannot atone for our sin by personal effort.

Let me illustrate for you how impossible it is for us to atone for our sin through good works. Let's say people who can jump from the East Coast of the United States to Europe will be forgiven of their sin and granted eternal life in heaven. We excitedly line up and give it our best running effort. Some people jump as hard as they can, and they only make it five feet before they land in the water. Some are better jumpers, and they make it ten feet before landing in the water. A professional athlete comes along and jumps farther than anyone; he makes it some thirty feet before falling into the water. The professional athlete can boast that he jumped farther than anyone; however, he is still over three thousand miles from Europe and remains as lost as the rest of us who could only jump five feet! That is exactly how it is when it comes to the idea of working our way to heaven. Some may look more religious than others. Some may live a more righteous life than others. Some may do more good works than others. Yet we are all missing heaven by an infinite distance because human effort cannot pardon our sin debt. The Bible tells us: "For all have sinned and come short of the glory of God" (Rom. 3.23). We all come short of God's perfect holiness, and there is nothing we can do about it. The truth is, we need someone to do for us what we cannot do for ourselves. That is where Jesus comes in. Jesus came to this earth in a human body and died for us on the cross of Calvary. Jesus did for us what we cannot do for ourselves. Jesus paid our sin debt in full.

What we are talking about here is the difference between genuine salvation by grace through faith and a presumed salvation by works. A works-based salvation is attractive to us because it makes us feel like we deserve to be forgiven. If we could do some good work, enter some lifestyle, or embrace a certain religion that atones for our sin, then God would be indebted to us. He would owe us heaven. God will never be indebted to anyone; He is God. Forgiveness of sin is received by grace through faith plus nothing. Grace is God's unmerited favor toward us. Grace is found in God doing for us what we cannot do for ourselves. Jesus Christ paid the penalty of our sin on the cross, which opened the way for God the Father to offer forgiveness and pardon to all who believe on Jesus by faith.

The Bible gives us the details behind salvation by grace through faith. The apostle Paul said, "But God commendeth his love toward us, in that, while we were yet sinners, Christ died for us. Much more then, being now justified by his blood, we shall be saved from wrath through him" (Rom. 5:8–9). Jesus was the sinless God-man. His death on the cross was sufficient to pay for the sin of the whole world. God the Father accepted the perfect sacrifice of His son on our behalf. By His sacrificial death on the cross, Jesus became both our representative and our substitute.[3] Adam was the first representative of all humanity who led us into sin and rebellion.

---

[3] Robert J. Utley, *The Gospel according to Paul: Romans*, vol. 5, Study Guide Commentary Series (Marshall, TX: Bible Lessons International, 1998), NP.

Jesus is the second Adam who purchased redemption for all humanity and leads us to righteousness and obedience. In the first Adam, all died a spiritual death—separation from God. In the second Adam, Jesus Christ, all who trust Him by faith are granted eternal spiritual life and eternal fellowship with the Father.

Salvation

Since Jesus paid for our sin, and God the Father is willing to forgive our sin and grant us eternal life, how does God's gift become our own? How does a lost person get saved? The answer is by faith. The pardon of sin and the receiving of God's eternal life happens when a lost person confesses his or her sin to God and places faith in Him. My own salvation is a good example. When I was eleven years old, my parents began to take me to church. To that point in my life I had not spent much time in church or under the hearing of the Bible. On one Sunday morning I was sitting in a Bible study class with a bunch of boys my age. Our teacher was an elderly woman who was faithfully teaching us God's Word. On this Sunday morning she asked those in the class who were sure they were saved to raise their hands. Everyone in the class raised their hands except for me. She turned to me and asked me point-blank if I was saved. I responded by telling her that I did not understand what she was asking; I did not know what it meant to be saved. This wonderful lady then proceeded to share with me the gospel of Jesus Christ. She explained that we are all sinners. She asked me if I was a sinner, and, of course, I responded in the affirmative. She then told me how Jesus is God's eternal Son, and He came here to die on the cross and pay for my sin. She told me how Jesus arose from the grave on the third day and is alive right now. She said if I was willing to confess my sin to God and by faith ask Jesus to forgive my sin and save my soul, He would save me in that moment. She asked me if I wanted to pray and ask Jesus to save me. I told her I wanted to pray, and she then said for me to pray out loud. I remember praying out loud that day, telling Jesus that I am a sinner and asking Him to forgive my sin and save my soul. I believed on Jesus that morning, and He saved me forever. There were no shinning lights, no earthquake, no superemotional experience—just a calm assurance that God did for me what He said He would do. I confessed my sin and by faith asked God to save me, and He did just that. I was saved the moment I placed my faith in Jesus. The words of the prayer were simply an outpouring of what was in my heart. I pray for you right now that you have the assurance of eternal life in Jesus. If you have never confessed your sin to God and by faith asked Jesus to save you, would you pause right now and take care of this most important decision? You can be eternally saved right now.

The Hidden Truth

If you have ever witnessed to someone about being saved by faith in Jesus, you have probably noticed how difficult it is to get lost people to understand. Even when we faithfully share the gospel with a lost person, it is often the case that they just don't get it. It is common that the lost person does not comprehend the need of a Savior. The lost person does not see the urgency of his or her lostness. The Bible explains this phenomenon to us by revealing that lost men and women have no capacity to understand God or His Word. The apostle Paul said that Satan has blinded the minds of those who are lost in their sin. He said, "But if our gospel be hid, it is hid to them that are lost: In whom the god of this world hath blinded the minds of them which believe not, lest the light of the glorious gospel of Christ, who is the image of God, should shine unto them" (2 Cor. 4:3–4). Sin blinds us to the truth of God's Word. It is only by the gracious power of the Holy Spirit that our minds and hearts are opened to the power of the gospel whereby we believe by faith and are saved.

This brings us back to our thoughts concerning what it means when we invite someone to be a follower of Christ. To invite someone to be a follower of Christ without sharing the gospel or dealing with their underlying sin issue is to invite a false religious experience. There is no salvation by association. A person is not saved by hanging around church or fellowshipping with saved people. There is no salvation by emotional experience. A person who is moved by the music or a compelling or sad story is not saved just because he or she cries or shouts. We have a biblical obligation to clearly articulate the necessity of being spiritually born again. If we stand before a crowd of people and in a general corporate sense invite them to be followers of Christ, we have done them a great disservice. At best we have committed a terrible oversight in our enthusiasm to grow the church, and at worst we have condemned them to a life of thinking they are right with God when they are not. It is interesting that the apostle Paul, the greatest missionary the world has ever known, never simply called people to be followers of Christ. Paul always led with the gospel message. His philosophy of evangelism and church growth are clearly set forth in Romans 1:16: "For I am not ashamed of the Gospel of Christ; for it is the power of God unto salvation to everyone what believeth; to the Jew first, and also to the Greek." For the apostle Paul the gospel of Christ was the instrument of evangelism whereby men and women become genuine followers of Christ.

Recently my wife and I were involved in our church's annual vacation Bible school (VBS). Every year we share the gospel with all the children, first through sixth grade. The older children—those who are between nine and twelve years old—usually have questions about Jesus and how to be saved. Those who wish to speak with someone about Jesus and what it means to be saved are spoken with on an individual basis. While my wife was talking to one of the young ladies about Jesus and what it means to be saved by faith, the young lady informed my wife that she had been baptized. She clearly equated water baptism with being saved. My wife asked the young lady if she knew what being baptized meant. She responded that she did not know. The young lady finally admitted that she was baptized simply because a bunch of her friends were doing it, and it seemed like the right thing to do. This young lady was caught up in the religious fervor of baptism and was never told how to truly be saved. Baptism is a testimony of having been saved by faith in Jesus. Baptism by immersion is a picture of dying with Jesus and then being resurrected with Him. No one has ever been saved by baptism; there is no salvation in the act. My wife had the privilege to share with this young lady how to be truly saved.

A second young lady was in the same spiritual darkness as the first. When my wife talked with her about Jesus, the young lady said that God just wants us all to be happy. In her mind, a relationship with God is measured by our perceived happiness. If I perceive things as going well in my life, then I must be right with God. If I fall on hard times, then I must not be right with God, and He must not love me. Nothing could be further from the truth. God is not nearly as concerned with our perceived happiness as He is with us being saved by faith in Jesus and obeying His Word. The interesting thing is that if we love God with all our hearts, souls, minds, and strength, we will discover true happiness is walking with Him, no matter our life circumstances. God's love for us transcends the temporal circumstances of this life. God's unconditional love for us is not connected to our happiness. This young lady is just another reminder that people have all kinds of ideas about God and their relationship to Him. Where did she learn these unbiblical views? Who knows, but it is our job to clearly articulate the truth of the gospel so that people may be truly saved by faith in Jesus and Him alone.

Nicodemus in the Dark

A biblical example of spiritual darkness is found in the story of a man named Nicodemus. Nicodemus was a religious scholar of his day—a Pharisee. Pharisees are often portrayed in a negative light when referred to in the New Testament; however, they were often the foremost examples of obedience to the law of Moses as well as being the primary interpreters of both the written law and oral traditions.[4] The conflict between Jesus and the Pharisees centered on their belief in works righteousness—a works-based salvation. The Pharisees had elevated their obedience of the law to a place of salvific effect. In other words, they thought they were acceptable before God based on their religious ethnic pedigree and good works. Thus, the stage was set for Nicodemus's encounter with Jesus.

We are told that Nicodemus came to Jesus at night. Opinions vary as to why he came to Jesus at night; however, it was most likely a strategic decision of convenience and opportunity. There would be fewer interruptions in the evening hours, which would afford a better opportunity for an in-depth discussion. Nicodemus said to Jesus, "Rabbi, we know that thou art a teacher come from God, for no man can do these miracles that thou doest, except God be with him" (John 3:2b). Nicodemus confessed two things in his address to Jesus. First, there seems to have been a group

---

[4] Marilyn J. Salmon, *Preaching without Contempt: Overcoming Unintended Anti-Judaism* (Minneapolis, MN: Fortress Press, 2006), 87.

of Pharisees within the religious leadership of Israel who were favorably disposed toward Jesus. These men had observed what Jesus was doing—the miracles and good works—and were convinced He was genuine. Not only did they observe what Jesus was doing; they listened to His teaching and were intrigued. Second, Nicodemus and his fellow Pharisees were sure Jesus was a man sent by God based on the amazing miracles Jesus was able to perform. No matter what a person may have thought of Jesus, it would have been difficult to ignore the fact that He was giving sight to the blind, causing the lame to walk, healing lepers, and even raising the dead. From an outward religious perspective, Nicodemus and his friends were followers of Christ. If we measured their followership of Jesus by today's standards, they would easily be included in most church circles as saved and on their way to heaven. Yet there were things about Jesus they did not understand. Nicodemus and his friends wanted to know more; in fact, they needed to know and confess more if they would become genuine followers of Christ.

The question Nicodemus intended to ask was never articulated; Jesus did not give him the opportunity to ask it. Jesus knew his question and provided the answer before it was asked. Jesus said, "Verily, verily, I say unto thee, except a man be born again, he cannot see the kingdom of God" (John 3:3b). It seems Nicodemus had a burning question concerning the kingdom of God. To fully grasp the power of what Jesus said, we need to understand what the term "kingdom of God" would have meant to Nicodemus and his friends. The Jews were looking for the Messiah who would deliver them from Roman dominion and bring in the promised kingdom—the son of David sitting on the throne of David forever (see Isa. 9:6–7). Nicodemus and his friends were looking for the arrival of the literal kingdom of God in the physical realm of the world in which they lived. Jesus's response to Nicodemus was designed to lift his thinking from the earthly to the heavenly, from militant religious law to a gracious spiritual kingdom. Nicodemus needed to understand that membership in the kingdom of God starts in the heart of man before it can be manifested externally in any way. To realize the kingdom he was looking for, Nicodemus needed to be born again by saving faith in Jesus as Lord and Savior. This point is critical to our thoughts concerning the church. Just as Nicodemus could have no part in a literal physical kingdom of God apart from saving faith in Jesus, so men and women today can have no part in a literal followership of Christ apart from first being saved by faith in Christ.

The evidence that Nicodemus's thinking was still operating in the earthly realm is seen in his reply: "How can a man be born when he is old? Can he enter the second time into his mother's womb, and be born?" (John 3:4b). Nicodemus's reply was no doubt rhetorical, but it demonstrated his lack of understanding nonetheless. Jesus had introduced the truth that His kingdom was both spiritual and physical. Nicodemus and his friends needed a spiritual new birth by faith in Jesus. Nicodemus and his friends could only be true followers of Jesus if they were born again by faith in Him. There is no entering the literal kingdom of God without first entering the spiritual kingdom of God by way of a spiritual new birth. Nicodemus and his friends may have passed on the outside as followers of Jesus, but Jesus identified the necessary change required in their hearts before they could be His true followers.

A False Security

What was true of Nicodemus and his friends is still true today. A lost man or woman has no capacity to be a follower of Jesus until he or she is saved by faith in Him and becomes a new creation in Christ by the power of the Holy Spirit. If lost people presume to be followers of Jesus in their lost condition, they simply enter into a religious exercise that has no eternal value. If we invite people to follow Jesus without first leading them to be saved, we run the very real danger of giving them a religious inoculation where they think they are saved and yet will perish in their sin without Jesus. If this view seems overdramatic, consider what Jesus said to His disciples concerning judgment day:

> Not everyone that saith unto me, Lord, Lord, shall enter into the kingdom of heaven; but he that doeth the will of my Father which is in heaven. Many will say to me in that day, Lord, Lord, have we not prophesied in thy name? and in thy name have cast out devils? and in thy name done many wonderful works? And then will I profess unto them, I never knew you: depart from me, ye that work iniquity. (Matt. 7:21–23)

Many will stand before Jesus on judgment day and proclaim they were His followers. They will claim as evidence of their followership all the religious things they did in Jesus's name. Sadly, however, Jesus will declare that He never knew them. Jesus will declare they were never saved by faith in Him; their sins had never been forgiven, and they were never born again. This is a sober warning from our Lord. The religious exercise of following Jesus has no salvific effect. Religious works cannot save us. I fear there are many in the professing Christian church today who fall under this scenario; they are religious in all the outward ways, but there has never been a time when they were born again by faith in Jesus. Many professing Christianity today will stand before Jesus one day only to hear Him say, "depart from me; I never knew you."

Perhaps the greatest example of one who was a follower of Jesus and yet never saved is Judas, one of Jesus's disciples. Judas was chosen by Jesus to be one of His twelve—the inner group who spent their lives with Jesus, engaged in the ministry. Think of what it must have been like to walk with Jesus and serve alongside Him in daily ministry. Judas was privileged to see the power of God firsthand as Jesus healed the sick, cast out demons, and even raised the dead. Judas sat under the hearing of Jesus's teaching every day, witnessing the crowds and those who were genuinely saved by faith in Him. Judas experienced the offer of God's unconditional love as Jesus gave him every opportunity to repent of his sin and be saved. Even after Judas betrayed Jesus and led the arrest party to the garden of Gethsemane, Jesus addressed Judas as friend, giving him one last opportunity to turn from his wickedness and be saved. Judas was by all outward appearances a follower of Jesus; he was among the twelves called by Jesus. Yet, we read in the Gospels how Judas's heart was given over to greed, stealing money from the group's purse, and then selling Jesus for thirty pieces of silver. Judas was a close follower of Jesus who never really knew Jesus.

If this kind of empty followership was present among the inner circle of Jesus's disciples, we can be sure it is present in the contemporary church of our day. There are people today who claim to be followers of Jesus, and they do not even know Him. The evidence is clear when we share the gospel with those around us. It is often the case that when I am talking to someone about Jesus, that person will claim to be a Christian. I might casually respond by asking the person to share with me his or her testimony. What circumstances brought the person to saving faith in Jesus? Did he or she pick up a Bible and read the gospel message? Was the individual in a church service where he or she heard the gospel presented by the preacher and trusted Jesus by faith? Did a friend or family member share the gospel with him or her? There are three responses I often hear that prove a lack of understanding and an empty followership of Christ.

Some will tell me they have always been saved. Maybe they grew up in a religious home or circle, and church is a way of life for them. The danger, however, is that they equate church attendance and participation with being saved. Remember, we have already seen that there is no one who is inherently righteous (Rom. 3:10). We are all born into this world with Adam's sin nature; we are naturally bent away from God by our fallen sin nature. No one is just automatically saved. If hanging around a bunch of saved people could save us, Judas would certainly have been saved; he was hanging around with Jesus and the other eleven in the inner circle. The truth is, salvation never happens by accident or by association. We are saved when we hear the gospel, the Holy Spirit draws us, and we volitionally confess our sin and ask Jesus to save us.

A second answer I often receive when I ask someone to give me his or her testimony has to do with the person's church denomination. The person will tell me he or she grew up Baptist, Methodist, Presbyterian, Pentecostal, Catholic, or some other affiliation. This is a clear indication that the person equates denominational affiliation with being saved. People think that because they are a member of a denomination, they must be okay with God. No one will ever be saved because he or she is of a particular denomination. Jesus made it clear when He said, "I am the way, the truth, and the life; no man cometh unto the Father, but by me" (John 14:6). Salvation comes by way of personal faith in Jesus; there is no other way.

Finally, there are those who trust in their good works to get them into haven. Some believe that when they stand before God, He will weigh their good works against their bad works, and if the good outweighs the bad, they are in. One man I spoke with was particularly adamant about this view. He declared quit forcefully that he was a good person, and God would never send him to hell. The problem is, we can never do enough good works to outweigh the debt of our sin. As previously pointed out, our very best effort is as rubbish before God. Isaiah the prophet said, "But we are all as an unclean thing, and all our righteousnesses are as filthy rags; And we all do fade as a leaf; And our iniquities, like the wind, have taken us away" (Isa. 64:4). The apostle Paul confirmed what Isaiah said: "Therefore by the deeds of the law there shall no flesh be justified in his sight: for by the law is the knowledge of sin" (Rom. 3.20). We conclude, then, that a man is saved by grace through faith in Jesus, completely apart from human effort or merit of any kind.

At the end of the day, God is the only one who knows if a person is saved or not because He is the only one who can see the heart of a human. There is no indication that the other eleven disciples knew Judas was a traitor who had never been saved. Likewise, there are professing Christians in the church today who have never been saved by grace through faith in Jesus. There are people who claim to be following Jesus for a variety of reasons and yet do not know Him. May we examine our own hearts and be sure we are in the faith. The apostle Paul said, "Examine yourselves, whether ye be in the faith" (2 Cor. 13:5a). Be sure that you are not a follower of Jesus in name only but that you have a genuine saving relationship with Him.

Easing the Sting of the Gospel

Over the last twenty or thirty years I have noticed a trend in contemporary evangelicalism. It seems there is a proliferation in presenting Jesus and the church using new terms, slogans, and phrases. It is almost as if we hired an advertising agency to survey the culture of our day and identify how to reach people. I have received postcards in the mail inviting me to attend a certain church and enjoy an elevated life. Others advertise a casual environment with coffee shops, the latest in music, Disney videos for the children, and a relevant message for the adults (as if every other church in the area has an irrelevant message). Terms such as "follower of Jesus" have become popular and are used often. It is as if the church is trying to be mainstream in our culture.

If the gospel is so straightforward, and it is, why has the church gone to this advertising agency approach? It is as if we think we must make the gospel relevant to our culture. It is as if the presentation of the gospel facts seems old-fashioned, and we need to help God come up with a newer and fresher way that will be more appealing to our contemporary culture. We have begun to major on the perceived contemporary benefits that God can bring to our lives, so that He seems attractive to the masses, while minoring on the most important part—how to be saved.

The church has begun to employ an entertainment-driven nonconfrontational approach to the gospel for the sake of perceived church growth. The number of people in the seats for a service, the size of the buildings, and the reports we can generate are all considered success. Asking someone to attend church and be a follower of Jesus sounds contemporary and appealing while at the same time taking the sting out of sharing the gospel. Asking someone to come to church and enjoy a choreographed service with high energy and a dynamic speaker is easy. In many pulpits, charisma and personality have replaced exposition of scripture and preaching in the power of the Holy Spirit.

Consider for a moment a comparison between the gospel message and simply calling people to follow Jesus for the perceived personal benefits. The gospel starts with our sin, which says we are the problem. The gospel calls us to decide between the world and God. The gospel confronts us with our helplessness in sin and calls us to accept God's way of salvation. The gospel makes us uncomfortable; it is convicting. We can talk about religion, we can talk about church, we can talk about denominations, we can even say to someone, "come follow Jesus," and all will be well. However, the moment we point out a personal sin problem, the moment we point out that we are all sinners in need of a Savior, it becomes uncomfortable and confrontational. I have never met a single lost person who likes being told he or she is a sinner. I have never met a single lost person who appreciates it when I recount what the Bible says about sin. Recently there was a lady who had been attending the church where I pastor. I noticed she had been absent from our services for a while, so I asked one of her family members if they knew why she stopped attending. Apparently, she was offended when we talked about sin; it made her feel uncomfortable and was too negative for her. This lady is a case in point. Lost people do not like to talk about sin. Being confronted by God over our sin is uncomfortable; it puts us on the horns of a dilemma. Do we confess our sin and ask for forgiveness, or do we continue in our rebellion against God and live life on our own terms? Every lost person who hears the gospel is faced with that decision, and it does not feel good. The gospel is the good news that Jesus saves. However, His salvation comes when we are willing to confess our sin to Him and by faith ask for His forgiveness.

Genie in the Bottle

The general call for people to be followers of Christ is not only less confrontational and thus more palatable to the lost; it also makes Jesus seem like the proverbial genie in the bottle. There is an ever-growing popularity of the prosperity gospel in our contemporary culture. There is the open call for people to be followers of Jesus based on what He can do for them here and now. The prosperity gospel either openly proclaims or subliminally insinuates that if a person becomes a follower of Christ, all his or her problems in this life will disappear. A person who professes to be a follower of Christ is somehow promised all the health, wealth, and fame that the heart desires. For example, a person who is struggling in his or her marriage might think, *Let me add some Jesus to my life so my marriage will be what I want it to be.* Perhaps another person is struggling financially, so that person thinks, *Let me add some Jesus to my life so my finances will be what I want them to be.* Yet another person is in poor health, so that person thinks, *I'll just add some Jesus to my life, so my health will be what I want it to be.* At the end of the day, all he or she is doing is adding some religion to an unrepentant sinful life. The lost person can easily be persuaded to make a religious connection to Jesus if we sell Jesus as the answer to all the problems in life and as the provider of all he or she wants in life. What person would not find it appealing to retain control of his or her life while adding Jesus for the supernatural blessings for success in the here and now? That is the message that is filling churches today with lost people who have a false hope in a false promise. There is no salvation in becoming a professed follower of Jesus where one simply adds Jesus as a religious aspect of life. True saving faith in Jesus entails a confession of sin with a repentant heart. We do not simply add Jesus to our lives; we surrender our lives to Him. True happiness in life—true contentment in life—can only be known when we confess our sin and surrender all to Jesus.

Summary

There is a prelude to be a true follower of Christ; a spiritual new birth is essential. There is no followership of Christ without first a relationship with Christ. Because of our inherent sin nature, we are naturally devoid of both a relationship with God and fellowship with God. Our sin stands as a wall between us and God. Why are we born into sin? Because Adam—the first man—disobeyed God and brought sin upon all humanity. Adam passed his sin nature to every generation of humanity that followed him. We are sinners by nature, and we are sinners by our own personal choices. The greatest need in every human life is to be redeemed from sin.

Fortunately for us, God the Father had a plan in place long before Adam sinned. God the Father planned to send His only begotten Son—Jesus Christ—to die on the cross as payment for our sin. The plan was for Jesus to take on the form of a man and experience death in our place. Because Jesus satisfied the penalty of sin on our behalf, we can by faith confess our sin to the Father and ask for His forgiveness. By saving faith in Jesus, our sin is forever removed from our account, and we are forever restored to a right relationship with God the Father. As a born-again child of God, we are now equipped by the power of the Holy Spirit to be a genuine follower of Jesus Christ. Inviting someone to follow Jesus by any other means is not only impossible; it is to invite much difficulty and spiritual deception. To be a true follower of Christ, one must be born again by grace through faith. How about you? Do you know Jesus as your personal Lord and Savior? If not, you can receive Him right now.

Two
APPRENTICESHIP

When I was a young man, just out of high school, I joined the navy. The navy sent me to an aviation electronics school where I was trained for over a year in all things electronic that might be found on an airplane. When I graduated from school, I was awarded the designation or technical rate of aviation electronics technician. I had the fancy title that said I was in the professional rate; however, I had never worked on an airplane in my young life. I was brand new to the rate; I had book knowledge but no experience fixing anything related to aviation electronics. When I arrived at my first duty station—a squadron of A-7E light attack aircraft—I realized I had a lot to learn. I quickly found a man in the shop who had been there for over a year. This man was highly skilled in troubleshooting and repairing aviation electronics on the A-7E aircraft. I told him that any time he left the shop to work on an airplane, I wanted to go with him. For the next several months I worked with this man and watched everything he did. I learned the tricks of the trade, as it were, by watching what he did and how he did it. I was his apprentice.

In many ways, being a follower of Christ is like my experience in the navy. The moment a person is saved by faith in Jesus, he or she becomes a member of the family of God. The moment a person has been born again by faith in Jesus, he or she is granted the title "child of God." The Holy Spirit bears witness to our spirit that we are genuinely saved, but the new convert knows little more than that. Being a follower of Christ is a lifelong learning process that begins with understanding what we have been called to be and do in the Christian life. The ongoing Christian life is a process of spiritual growth whereby we become more mature in our faith and express that maturity by an ever-increasing conformity to the image of Christ. In other words, just like an apprentice who learns from the master, we are called to learn from our Master by examining and understanding how He lived when He was here. How do learn of Jesus? How do we observe our Master and emulate Him when we can't see or observe His life? We learn of Jesus by reading the Bible. We are conformed to the image of Christ by the power of the Holy Spirit when the Word of God is applied to our heart. In other words, the Bible is a living book, empowered by the Holy Spirit to the changing of human hearts. The Bible is the written Word that reveals to us the living Word, Jesus Christ.

Since we are to follow the example of Jesus, we might ask, what exactly does that mean? We find a specific answer to that question in a conversation Jesus had with His disciples. As Jesus drew near the cross, He informed His disciples that His death was imminent. Jesus was specific in foretelling His death, laying out for them how He would suffer at the hands of the religious leaders and be killed. Jesus even foretold His resurrection, telling them He would be raised again the third day. This news of Jesus's death did not sit well with Peter. Peter pulled Jesus aside and rebuked Him. Peter could not comprehend how Jesus would allow Himself to be killed. Matthew records the account, including Jesus's follow-on instruction concerning what it means to be His follower.

> From that time forth began Jesus to shew unto his disciples, how that he must go unto Jerusalem, and suffer many things of the elders and chief priests and scribes, and be killed, and be raised again the third day. Then Peter took him, and began to rebuke him, saying, be it far from thee, Lord: this shall not be unto thee. But he turned, and said unto Peter, get thee behind me, Satan: thou art an offence unto me: for thou savourest not the things that be of God, but those that be of men. Then said Jesus unto his disciples, if any man will come after me, let him deny himself, and take up his cross, and follow me. For whosoever will save his life shall lose it: and whosoever will lose his life for my sake shall find it (Matt. 16:21–25).

In this passage, Jesus identified three character traits of the person who would be a genuine follower of Him. These character traits are not optional; they are essential for all who desire to follow Christ. Remember, being an apprentice means doing what we see the Master do. Jesus said His followers must do what He did. The three character traits we are to emulate include denying self, taking up our cross, and following. Let's think about what each of these requirements mean in our lives as followers of Christ.

Deny Self

The first character trait necessary for being a follower of Christ is self-denial. This is not a legalistic practice of outward religious conformity; rather this is a willing submission to the person and power of Jesus in one's life. Denying self involves willing conformity to all things that emulate Jesus and bring glory to His name. Warren Wiersbe summarized the idea when he said, "It means to give yourself wholly to Christ and share in His shame and death."[5] To give ourselves wholly to Christ by necessity means we surrender self-control and self-determination as concerns the manner of life we live after we are saved. The idea of self-denial is antithetical to the contemporary culture of our day. In fact, we could accurately describe the contemporary culture of our day as the "me" generation. We live in a culture where each person lives as if he or she is the center of the universe. Every decision, every action, and every interaction with others seems to be focused on the advancement of personal goals and the achievement of self-actualization. To be a follower of Jesus means to forsake such a self-centered lifestyle. To be a follower of Jesus means a willingness to set aside personal desires and goals to be a part of the plan and will of God for our lives. Hendriksen connected the idea of denying self to a separating of ourselves from the old person that identified who we were before we were saved.[6] In other words, denying self is in accord with the apostle Paul's

---

[5] Warren W. Wiersbe, *The Bible Exposition Commentary* (Wheaton, IL: Victor Books, 1996), 60.

[6] William Hendriksen, *New Testament Commentary: Matthew* (Grand Rapids, MI: Baker Books, 2002), 656.

instruction to put off the old man and put on the new man in Christ (Eph. 4:22). To live as a follower of Christ means to let Him lead.

Denying self not only deals with a willing submission to Christ, but it also deals with our ongoing temptation to sin as well. The unregenerate flesh of man is easily smitten by sinful desires that hold the promise of satisfying man's baser lustful cravings. Sin appeals to our self-first nature. Sin always holds the allure of ultimate happiness and satisfaction. To deny self means dealing decisively with habitual sin. To be a follower of Christ means turning from sin and embracing holiness. It is completely incongruous for a person to profess followership of Christ while at the same time living in known unrepentant sin. As the apostle Paul said, "What communion hath light with darkness" (2 Cor. 6:14)? Being saved by faith in Jesus does not make us practically perfect in this life, for we still live in unregenerate flesh. However, all who are saved by faith in Jesus are permanently indwelt by God the Holy Spirit, who is more than powerful enough to give us victory over every temptation that we genuinely resist. James said, "Submit yourselves therefore to God. Resist the devil, and he will flee from you" (James 4.7). The problem in the church today is a lack of genuine resisting. Rather than run from sin, there are too many professed followers of Christ standing around waiting for sin to catch up with them. Denying self means denying the sinful lust of the flesh and following Jesus in purity and integrity. Denying self means being yielded to God. We must choose who we will serve. Allowing sin is the same as being ruled by sin, rather than serving God (Rom. 6:11–12).

If being a follower of Christ involves denying self, what has happened to the church in the affluent culture of the United States of America? I believe the church is infected with the same self-centered sinful paradigm of the lost worldly culture around us. Preaching from the pulpits of America has increasingly become about the here and now. The emphasis seems to have shifted from the self-denial call of Christ to a message that promises blessings, success, happiness, and grandeur in this life. Nowhere in the Bible—and I mean nowhere—is it even intimated that when we are born again by faith in Jesus, we will somehow experience our best life in the here and now. There is no such thing for the child of God as experiencing our best life now. Much to the contrary, the apostle Paul reminded his young protégé, Timothy: "Yea, and all what will live godly in Christ shall suffer persecution" (2 Tim. 3.12). I believe preaching, in many instances, has shifted to a more crowd-pleasing flavor for the sole purpose of being more palatable to the hearers and thus more likely to result in bigger crowds on Sunday morning. Many will gladly gather to hear a message that panders to their self-centered worldview and selfish desires. Many will come and sit in the service for one hour a week if the preacher promises them God's blessings and makes them feel good about their self-centered plans and lifestyle. The apostle Paul warned Timothy of this very thing: "For the time will come when they will not endure sound doctrine; but after their own lusts shall they heap to themselves teachers, having itching ears; And they shall turn away their ears from the truth, and shall be turned unto fables" (2 Tim. 4.3). It is nothing short of false doctrine to preach that it is God's purpose for Christians to enjoy an easy and prosperous life in this world. By God's grace we may indeed enjoy relative ease and even a measure of worldly prosperity, but these things are given to us by God to be employed in doing His will. This life is not about us; it is all about Jesus.

The greatest example of what it means to deny self is found in the person of our Savior—Jesus Christ. The apostle Paul urged the church at Philippi to adopt the very attitude of Jesus concerning self-denial and willing sacrifice.

> Let this mind be in you, which was also in Christ Jesus:
> Who, being in the form of God, thought it not robbery
> to be equal with God: But made himself of no reputation,
> and took upon him the form of a servant, and was made in
> the likeness of men: And being found in fashion as a man,
> he humbled himself, and became obedient unto death,
> even the death of the cross (Phil. 2:5–8).

Jesus thought it not robbery to be equal with God for He is the eternal God. Jesus is the eternal God—the one who deserves all the glory. Yet Jesus was willing to lay aside His rightful glory as God to take on the form of a servant. The word for servant is *doulos*, which means a slave who is completely under the control of another. Jesus willingly humbled Himself to take on a human body and ultimately die on the cross as payment for the sin of the world. Jesus denied Himself in obedience to God the Father and became sin in our place. Jesus took our death, so we could have His life. Those who are followers of Christ are to emulate His self-denial as we live in obedience to God the Father. We are to let the mind of Christ be in us as we live for Him. The apostle Paul understood this principle as he often referred to himself as the servant of the Lord. Paul used the same word, *doulos,* concerning his surrender to God's call upon his life. Paul considered himself a slave of Jesus, one compelled by grace to completely surrender to His will in this life. Unfortunately, much of Christendom today knows little of this kind of surrendered life to Christ. Christianity today holds very little likeness to the Pauline theology of servanthood, let alone the idea of complete surrender as indicated by the word *doulos.* May we as true followers of Jesus surrender completely to the control and leadership of our Lord and Savior.

Cross Bearing

The second character trait necessary for being a follower of Christ is cross bearing. Jesus said we are not only to deny self, but we are to take up our cross as we follow Him. For the Jews of Jesus's day, the cross was a visible and literal emblem of suffering and death. Just as recorded in the events of Jesus's death, those condemned to die by means of crucifixion were often forced to carry their own crosses to the place of execution. This statement by our Lord is a call for His followers to be willing to suffer at whatever level is required to remain true to Him. No two followers of Jesus are called to serve in the same capacity; however, all are called to serve with the same surrender, diligence, and commitment. Cross bearing is a continual willingness to pay whatever price is required to remain true to Jesus—even to the point of sacrificing our physical lives if called upon to do so. John MacArthur said it this way: "To come to Jesus Christ is to come to the end of self and sin and to become so desirous of Christ and His righteousness that one will make any sacrifice for Him."[7] We might ask ourselves, how much do we desire the righteousness of Christ? Do we indeed wish to be more like Jesus, or are we just playing a religious game

---

[7] John MacArthur, *The MacArthur New Testament Commentary: Matthew 16–23* (Chicago, IL: Moody Press, 1988), 49.

that will come to a tragic end one day? There seems to be a shortage of Christians in the contemporary church of today who are willing to carry their crosses.

The reality of Christian cross bearing is most clearly seen in the historical record of the early church fathers of the first century church. Ignatius, bishop of Antioch, for example, was arrested by the Romans in 110 AD for being a Christian and refusing to worship the pagan Roman gods.[8] He was carried to Rome in chains, bound to a Roman soldier throughout the journey. The exact record and details of his death are lost to time; however, his letters to Polycarp clearly reveal he anticipated being fed to wild animals in the colosseum of Rome.[9] Polycarp himself would later suffer martyrdom for his faith, being burned alive at the stake for refusing to renounce the name of Christ. The willingness—dare we say anticipation—of early Christians to suffer for the name of Jesus reveals an incredible dichotomy between those early Christians and what one finds in Christianity today. Rather than a willingness to pursue Christ at all costs, one finds in the contemporary church a clear focus on self—the pleasures of the flesh, the comforts of the flesh, and personal gratification through the collection of this world's trinkets. Even within the professing church itself, Christians are more concerned with personal preferences in worship style, personal agendas concerning clothing styles, new church models, and boldly living as close to the world as possible without completely disavowing Christ. At a recent gathering of leaders in a prominent Christian denomination, one leader was heard boasting that he enjoyed drinking a beer from time to time and had no problem letting his church and others know about it. Before we get carried away boasting of our Christian liberty in Christ, we would do well to remind ourselves how the apostle Paul was willing to forsake any and every Christian liberty in his life so that he would not become a stumbling block to weaker brothers in Christ or the lost (see 1 Cor. 8:13). The apostle Paul was always willing to temper his liberty in Christ for the benefit of winning others to faith

---

[8] David DeSilva, *An Introduction to the New Testament Contexts, Methods, and Ministry Formation* (Downers Grove, IL: InterVarsity Press, 2004), 755.
[9] Robert Grant, "Polycarp of Smyrna," *Anglican Theological Review* 28, no. 3 (1946): 138.

in Christ, so they might be saved. The point is, there is very little genuine cross bearing taking place in the church today.

Taking up our cross and following Jesus entails this life becoming less about us and more about Him. We must ask ourselves if we are willing to set aside the cultural norms of an increasingly wicked secular society so that we might present ourselves before Jesus as an instrument fit for His use. Are we willing to take personal inventory of our lives and set aside any habit or lifestyle that would inhibit our full surrender and devotion to Christ? The apostle Paul addressed this very matter when he said to Timothy:

> Nevertheless the foundation of God standeth sure, having this seal, The Lord knoweth them that are his. And, let every one that nameth the name of Christ depart from iniquity. But in a great house there are not only vessels of gold and of silver, but also of wood and of earth; and some to honour, and some to dishonour. If a man therefore purge himself from these, he shall be a vessel unto honour, sanctified, and meet for the master's use, and prepared unto every good work. (2 Tim. 2:19–21)

Paul gave two exhortations in this passage—two things we are responsible for doing in our own lives. First, we are to depart from iniquity. To depart from iniquity means to abstain from evil and to remove from one's life those things that are unrighteous, those things that offend God, and those things that will hinder our walk and service to Him. The positive perspective is to actively pursue holiness and obedience to God's Word and will for our lives. The second exhortation is a follow on to the first; we are to purge ourselves, so we might be a vessel of honor, fit for the Master's use. Being used of God begins with a heart that desires holiness. Being used of God begins with knowing how to confess our sin and pray for God's sustaining power to walk holy before Him.

Cross bearing is deeper and broader than many Christians understand or care to embrace. It is, however, what we are called to do if we would be genuine followers of Christ. We need to examine our own hearts and determine if we are willing to purge ourselves of everything that might defile us, dishonor us, or bring reproach on the name of Jesus. Cross bearing cannot be forced upon a person by legalism. A willing cross bearing for Christ comes from a new heart; this kind of cross bearing is a result of an ever-increasing spiritual walk with Jesus in the power of the Holy Spirit. To take up our cross and follow Jesus is a personal choice, which is then empowered and enabled by the Holy Spirit. The problem is, few are truly willing to take up their crosses and follow Jesus.

Follow Me

The final character trait of a follower of Christ is the cognitive volitional decision to follow Him. Following Jesus is not compulsory; it is a choice that God allows each person to freely make. Jesus said, "If any man will come after me" (Matt. 16:24). The decision to follow Jesus is one of conscious reasoning whereby the facts are examined, which then brings one to a determined course of action. What kind of facts influence the decision to follow Jesus? The first influence comes from the reality of a new spiritual relationship with Him. As pointed out in the previous chapter, the precursor to be a follower of Jesus is the spiritual new birth by grace through faith in Jesus. The illuminating work of the Holy Spirit opens our minds and understanding to the reality of what Jesus has done for us. His sacrifice on our behalf influences us to follow Him out of gratitude for His great mercy and grace. Every born-again child of God owes Jesus everything. By His blood we were redeemed—purchased from the slavery of sin and death. Through faith in Jesus we have eternal life. We who are saved not only choose to follow Jesus because of His saving love for us; we are compelled by His mercy and grace to lay ourselves on the altar as a living sacrifice to Him. The apostle Paul said it this way: "I beseech you therefore, brethren, by the mercies of God, that ye present your bodies a living sacrifice, holy, acceptable unto God, which is your reasonable service. And be not conformed to this world: but be ye transformed by the renewing of your mind, that ye may prove what is that good, and acceptable, and perfect, will of God" (Rom. 12:1–2). Considering all Jesus has done for us, it is only reasonable that we present ourselves a living sacrifice to Him.

The second influence upon the Christian's life in deciding to follow

Jesus comes from the Word of God—the Bible. The more we read and study the Bible, the more we are matured in our faith and walk in this world. As an apprentice one must study the craft that he or she seeks to master. This principle is no less true in the Christian life. The apostle Paul said to Timothy: "Study to shew thyself approved unto God, a workman that needeth not to be ashamed, rightly dividing the word of truth" (2 Tim. 2:15). The word *study* is the Greek word *spoudazo*, which means to be eager or zealous in one's effort. If a Christian is to be an apprentice or follower of Jesus Christ, effort must be invested. Specifically, effort must be invested in knowing the Bible, so we might rightly perceive the difference between truth and error. We cannot be a follower of Jesus apart from consistent study and understanding of the Bible. The Bible has the inherent power to be an incredible influence upon our lives if we will but read it. Not only read it but give due diligence to understand and apply it practically to our lives.

The reason we are to give such diligence to studying the Bible is so that we might be able to present ourselves before God as approved. The word *approved* means one who has been tested and proven reliable and dependable. An apprentice is not much of an apprentice if that person never progresses in his or her abilities to a point where the individual can be trusted to do the job. When we become followers of Jesus, we become laborers together with Him. Paul used the word *workman*. There is no place for laziness in the Christian life. As apprentices of our Lord, we are to labor—work hard—at learning all we can about Him, so we might serve Him and not be ashamed.

What is the ultimate goal of all our hard work? We are to learn how to handle the Word of God accurately. The phrase Paul used—"rightly dividing the word of truth"—literally means to cut straight. The phrase might be applied to plowing a straight row in a field or cutting material in a straight line. We are to prepare ourselves as followers of Christ, so we can cut straight with God's Word. We are to be prepared to handle God's Word accurately. As we earnestly study the Word of God, we find we are not only prepared to be good workers in the labor of our Lord, but we are increasingly conformed to His image in our own daily lives. As a follower of Jesus, we are His apprentices, learning to live and do what He did in life and in the ministry. The Word of God equips us to do the work of the

Christian life. We are not just equipped but thoroughly equipped—fully equipped to do the work God has called us to in this life. The only thing that hinders us from being diligent students of God's Word is the lack of conscious choice to do so.

A third influence upon the Christian to follow Jesus comes by way of fellowship in a local biblically based congregation. The church of Jesus Christ is universal. That means all who are saved by faith in Jesus are part of the family of God, united by our common spiritual birth. We are encouraged in our followership of Jesus when we are united with a local church body where we share in ministry and accountability among one another. The writer to the Hebrews said, "And let us consider one another to provoke unto love and to good works: Not forsaking the assembling of ourselves together, as the manner of some is; but exhorting one another: and so much the more, as ye see the day approaching" (Heb. 10:24–25). In the local church assembly, we are provoked—encouraged by the testimony of others—to follow and serve Jesus. As we associate with other Christians who are employing their spiritual gifts in service to our Lord, we are motivated to do the same. We see here the specific instruction against forsaking the assembly of believers. If we desire to be genuine followers of Jesus, we need the positive influence that comes with participation in the corporate worship and ministry of a local church body.

Since being saved and following Jesus is a cognitive decision, made in the power of the Holy Spirit, how do contemporary ideas of choosing to follow Jesus line up? Choosing to follow Christ, particularly by those who have never been born again, is often induced by an emotional plea. In many contemporary settings, the process of sharing the gospel verbally to bring conviction over sin and ultimately saving faith in Christ has been replaced with high-powered emotional programs that move people with a desire to be a part of something exciting. Many contemporary church services have become well-orchestrated productions that capture and titillate the senses, creating an atmosphere of excitement and exuberance. This high-powered emotional experience is followed by a plea from a charismatic leader to raise the hand or come forward if you want to be a follower of Christ. For the lost person, following Christ has, in that setting, been equated with feelings of excitement, belonging, and encouragement, which most people desire to feel as often as possible. The result is that the lost person raises his or her hand and comes forward or joins the church. The lost person is now a member of the church; that person thinks he or she is saved and returns every Sunday morning to get an emotional fix for the next week. That scenario is exacerbated by weekly feel-good messages that never mention sin, never warn of eternal hell, and never deal with any biblical passage that even approaches a negative thought. The focus of such a church setting is to provide weekly pep talks and make the congregants feel good about themselves and their lives.

Lest I be accused of denying the joy of being saved, let me say I fully embrace an upbeat worship service and the expression of joy in knowing and worshipping our great God. The psalmist wrote, "O come, let us sing unto the Lord: Let us make a joyful noise to the rock of our salvation" (Ps. 95:1). Those who are truly saved by faith in Jesus have an inner joy that cannot be diminished by the cares, trials, and tribulations of this life. Those who are truly saved are free to express their love and worship to God in many various ways. A worship service that truly points out and exalts the greatness of our God should not be like entering a morgue. However, seeking to build and sustain large crowds through well-choreographed performance-centered services can quickly get off track. The greatest danger is that we would convince lost people that they are now followers of Christ when in fact they have never been born again. They have never been born again because they were never presented with a clear proclamation of the gospel by which they were convinced to make a cognitive decision to confess their sin and ask for God's forgiveness and saving grace. A true follower of Christ is one who has made a cognitive response to the call of the Holy Spirit upon his or her heart. Emotion may accompany a salvation experience, but emotion is certainly not the driving factor. The late great preacher Adrian Rogers once pointed out that our emotions are the shallowest part of our being. He went on to say that God would never deal with our greatest need—to be forgiven of our sin—through the shallowest part of our being. Salvation and authentic followership of Christ are the result of genuine conviction over sin and a subsequent cognitive decision to confess our sin with a repentant heart and by faith ask for His forgiveness.

Summary

We began this chapter by using the metaphor of apprenticeship to describe what it means to be a follower of Christ. An apprentice watches the master, follows the master, emulates the master, and seeks to be like the master in every way. Is that an accurate description of your life? Can you look back on your life and see a time when you confessed your sin to God and by faith asked Jesus to forgive you and save your soul? There is no salvation in church membership, good works, denominational affiliation, or family heritage. True saving faith is a personal transaction between each individual and God. The apostle Paul said it this way: "That if thou shalt confess with thy mouth the Lord Jesus, and shalt believe in thine heart that God hath raised him from the dead, thou shalt be saved. For with the heart man believeth unto righteousness; and with the mouth confession is made unto salvation" (Rom. 10:9–10). What a glorious and gracious offer God extends to each of us.

As a follower of Christ, we are called to make a definitive decision to deny self, take up our crosses, and follow Him. We must be willing to make a clear and clean break with this world and turn all our attention to following the Master. We must deal daily with the weakness of the flesh—living in the power of the indwelling Holy Spirit. We must continue to live for Jesus when the path He has chosen for us becomes difficult or challenging. We must make a cognitive decision to be a follower of Christ and then do all in our power to remove any and all hindrances to that purpose. As a child of God, we are called to be followers of Jesus. Today is a good day to begin.

Three

GROWTH

On December 18, 1992, my daughter, Meagan, was born into our family. There was great joy with her birth, and we celebrated and thanked God. However, the journey to her arrival had not been easy and was fraught with much peril. My wife's pregnancy had been incredibly difficult. Early in the pregnancy my wife was deemed at risk for a variety of medical reasons, which in turn placed Meagan's life at risk as well. Meagan was born almost four weeks early, and she was the tiniest person I had ever seen. She was so small at birth that I could literally hold her in one hand with no danger of her falling out. The miraculous part is that when she was born, her lungs were fully functional, and there was no requirement to put her on any kind of breathing machine. Not only were her lungs working perfectly; the rest of her, though very small, functioned normally as well. God had graciously answered many prayers on her behalf.

On the day Meagan was born an amazing thing began to happen; she was hungry and wanted to eat. Her eating supported a process of growth that encompassed her entire person—physically, mentally, and spiritually. Meagan had an appetite that drove her to seek out food, which in turn caused her to grow. Meagan is full grown now; she is a beautiful mature married woman. She loves her husband; she works a full-time job, and she serves the Lord in their local church. Her birth into our family was just the beginning; she is now an adult who exhibits all the attributes of a godly Christian woman.

Becoming a follower of Christ is in many ways like being born physically into this world. A baby is born into this world with an appetite. As the baby eats, beginning with milk and progressing to ever increasing levels of solid food, a growth process takes place. The growth process eventually leads to maturity and full functionality in society. A new Christian is a spiritual babe in Christ. The apostle Peter said, "As newborn babes, desire the sincere milk of the word, that ye may grow thereby" (1 Pet. 2:2). Just like a physical baby, the new spiritual babe in Christ will have a God-given hunger for spiritual food whereby he or she will grow spiritually and become a mature functioning member of the body of Christ. A Christian who fails to feed the spiritual man or woman will be spiritually weak and susceptible to all sorts of deception, false teaching, and sin. There is no spiritual growth apart from the Word of God that nourishes the soul.

Unlike growth in the physical realm, we who are saved never stop growing spiritually—spiritual growth is a lifelong process. A growing Christian should reach a place of spiritual maturity; however, we never arrive at some point of spiritual completion in this life. In other words, the follower of Christ never reaches a place of practical sinless perfection in this life. There is coming a day when Jesus will give us a resurrection body like His, and we will be removed from the very presence and temptation of sin. When we receive our resurrection body, we will then be practically sinless. In our mortal unredeemed flesh, we feed on God's Word and rely completely on the power of the Holy Spirit as we follow Jesus.

The importance of spiritual growth in the Christian life cannot be overstated. We have seen that there are two kinds of people in the world—those who are saved by faith in Jesus and those who are lost in their sin. There are those who are regenerate in Christ, and there are those who are unregenerate; they are outside of Christ. Among those who are regenerate—saved by faith—there are two further categories. There are those followers of Christ who are growing and walking spiritually in this life, and there are those followers of Christ who are not growing and who are walking in accord with this world. The apostle Paul used the word *carnal* to describe Christians who are walking in the power and influence of the flesh. In one of his letters to the church at Corinth, Paul said, "And I, brethren, could not speak unto you as unto spiritual, but as unto carnal, even as unto babes in Christ. I have fed you with milk, and not with meat: for hitherto ye were not able to bear it, neither yet now are ye able" (1 Cor. 3:1–2). The word *carnal* in Paul's letter to the Corinthian Christians is the Greek word *sarkikós*, which one author astutely defined as being made of or originating from a heart of flesh.[10] A carnal Christian can therefore be described as a person who has genuinely been born again by faith in Jesus but is living under the influence of the sinful and fallen fleshly nature. The Christians in Corinth were genuinely saved—indwelt by the Holy Spirit; however, they were living defeated lives under the power and persuasion of their fleshly lusts and selfishness. What a sad state of existence for any true child of God. The Lord Jesus saved us and set us free from the bondage and slavery of sin. The apostle Paul said, "For the law of the Spirit of life in Christ Jesus hath made me free from the law of sin and death" (Rom. 8:2). How sad that one who has been redeemed from the curse and power of sin by the blood of Jesus would again turn back to following that which had enslaved and doomed his or her soul.

The path to becoming and sustaining a growing followership of Jesus is found in the fundamental practices of the Christian life. There are three foundational practices that should be true in every Christian life. First, if the child of God desires to be a growing follower of Christ, spiritual nourishment is required. The Bible—the Word of God—is the nourishment we must consume daily. God the Holy Spirit uses the Word of God to teach us, correct us, and make us wise in recognizing truth from error. The second foundational practice for spiritual growth is regular communion with our heavenly Father through prayer. Praying Christians are growing Christians. Third, spiritual growth is sustained and enhanced by active participation in a local body of believers. It is in the local church setting where the child of God can employ his or her individual and unique spiritual gifts for the edification of others. As we serve others, we reap the benefit of spiritual growth. Let's consider these three elements of spiritual growth in more detail.

Spiritual Nourishment

It has often been said of the human body that we are what we eat. Too much pizza and too many hamburgers, french fries, and sodas will

---

[10] Robert James Utley, *Paul's Letters to a Troubled Church: I and II Corinthians*, vol. 6, Study Guide Commentary Series (Marshall, TX: Bible Lessons International, 2002), 42.

adversely affect our health and pants size! The principle is likewise true of the spiritual person we are in Christ. Spiritual growth, health, and vitality are all directly connected to the spiritual nourishment we consume. It is impossible to grow spiritually as a follower of Christ apart from a steady diet of God's Word. The apostle Paul addressed this very issue with the young preacher Timothy. Paul said, "All scripture is given by inspiration of God, and is profitable for doctrine, for reproof, for correction, for instruction in righteousness: That the man of God may be perfect, thoroughly furnished unto all good works" (2 Tim. 3:16–17). Much like the nutritional factor of the food we eat to sustain and maintain the health of our physical bodies, the apostle Paul identified five benefits of the Word of God in the spiritual life of the growing follower of Christ.

First, we see that the Word of God is powerful because it is inspired. We find here the apostle Paul's reminder to Timothy concerning the origin of all scripture. The word *inspiration* is the Greek word *theopneustos*, which means God breathed. It is a compound word containing *theos*, which means God, and *pneuma*, which means spirit or breath. God the Holy Spirit superintended, oversaw, and directed the writing of the Bible. The men whom God moved to pen the words of the Bible were supernaturally directed within their own individual education, vocabulary, and experience in life. All of scripture—the entire Bible—is God's supernatural revelation of Himself to man, and it is God's message to all of humanity. Because of its divine origin, the Bible is inherently endued with binding authority. One intuitively recognizes that God has the right to establish and convey His wishes and commands concerning the way we as His created creatures should live in His world. The Bible is divinely authoritative and serves as the source of knowledge concerning salvation. The Bible is the standard of life for every generation of humanity.

Regarding Christian living, the Bible is the absolute standard. The Bible is often referred to as the canon or closed canon of God's revelation to man. The word *canon* comes to us through the Latin language, originating with the Greek word *kanon*. The Greek word means a rod or straight stick used as a ruler.[11] As such, the Bible is the standard by which we measure life. To know about God, we read the Bible. To know where we came from,

---

[11] F. F. Bruce, *The Canon of Scripture* (Downers Grove, IL: InterVarsity Press, 1988), 17.

we read the Bible. To know the purpose of life, we read the Bible. To know the moral boundaries of this life, we read the Bible. To know how we are to live as the redeemed of Christ, we read the Bible. To know what happens when this life is over, we read the Bible. The Bible is the sole source of all we need to know about God and the Christian life. We understand, then, how the follower of Christ has no hope of imitating the nature and life of Christ apart from measuring one's life against scripture. The New Testament reveals the life of Jesus in the Gospels. The epistles of the New Testament lay the foundational instruction of what the Christian life should look like as one lives in a lost world and serves in the local church body. The Bible is the only source from which a follower of Christ can receive instruction that is profitable for the Christian life. How disastrous for the follower of Christ is a laissez-faire attitude toward the Bible. The Bible serves as a spiritual mirror by which we might gaze upon our spiritual reflection and see where our spiritual lives need attention. It is impossible to be an apprentice of Jesus—one who professes to be a follower of Christ—and never spend time in the Word of God. The Bible is the singular authoritative source whereby we can measure the world around us and then by the discernment of the Holy Spirit make good choices in our personal lives. Absolute truth is a reality, and we find it in the pages of scripture.

I remember being in a meeting one time where I was rebuked by one of our deacons for allowing the worship leader to lead the congregation in worship without a tie on. This brother in Christ was an older man who had been a Christian for a long time. He proceeded to give me all the reasons why it was scandalous—downright disrespectful to God and His church—for such a thing to be allowed. The tieless worship leader was not the only thing on his mind; he then told me and the rest of the men in the meeting that the drums were too loud and had no place in the music program. I will not bore you with all the details of how the rest of that meeting went, but you can see that I was having a joyous time up to that point! The brother's motive and sincerity were not the problem. He genuinely believed everything he was saying, and he believed it with a passion. The problem was his spiritual immaturity. There was not one shred of biblical basis for his objections; they were all personal preference. He was a longtime Christian who was a babe in Christ. In fact, he should not have been serving as a deacon; he was not spiritually mature enough.

The Bible must be our standard for all things, and when it is, there is unity. When personal preference becomes the standard, there will always be confusion and discord.

After telling us the Bible is the ruler for all of life, Paul then reminds us that the Bible contains doctrine. When Paul said that all scripture is good for doctrine, he was referring to the value of scripture for teaching. The word for doctrine is *didaskalia*, which means teaching or instructing. The one who reads the Bible or sits under its oft-repeated precepts learns the essential truths needed to live out the Christian life in the power of the Holy Spirit. It has been said that good doctrine—a continual exposure to biblical teaching and instruction—brings stability to the Christian life.[12] Stability in the Christian life means consistency—the habit of one's walk with the Lord. To be a follower of Jesus one needs stability; that is, a consistent lifestyle of conformity to the image of Christ. Through a steady influence of the Word of God one learns self-discipline and surrender to the direction and influence of the Holy Spirit. Apart from learning God's Word there is no true discipleship or followership of Jesus. Good doctrine is invaluable to the Christian life.

I was recently perusing the web site of a church that had been brought to my attention as having an impressive website design. It was indeed an impressive website, one that caused me to rethink how our own church website looks and how we might make a better presentation in our community via that outreach tool. As I clicked on the various tabs, I came to a tab that said, "doctrinal statement." When the tab opened, my heart sank at what I read there. This church declared on its website that they did not have a doctrinal statement because it was too divisive. They went on to say they would rather focus on unity around Christ than be divided by doctrine. In the mind of that pastor and church leadership, that declaration may sound profoundly spiritual, enlightened, and even groundbreaking as they seek to avoid offending anyone. I can't help but wonder, though, how they get around what Paul said to Timothy in this text. If we are to teach God's Word, His precepts, and His instruction for our lives, doctrine is essential. If we do not stand firm on God's inerrant infallible Word, we will simply be like a ship adrift in the ocean with no direction. Good doctrine

---

[12] Henry Alford, *Alford's Greek Testament: An Exegetical and Critical Commentary* (Grand Rapids, MI: Guardian Press, 1976), 397.

means teaching God's people the truth of what God has said in His Word. We cannot be followers of Christ without good doctrine.

Doctrine is not only valuable for consistency in one's Christian walk; it is the source and foundation of our personal convictions. The Bible is the standard by which we measure all of life. As we learn the Word of God, we gain wisdom and discernment—the ability to measure accurately between right and wrong. Our personal convictions come in two categories—those founded on the law of God and those we choose by personal preference. The moral law of God's Word should be the foundation of undisputed convictions in our lives. For example, we prayerfully abstain from lying and seek to be truthful in all things because God said we are not to lie. We prayerfully seek to have a pure heart in the area of sexuality because God said it is a sin to commit fornication or adultery. The law of God should be the standard for which we constantly strive. Not because it is legally required but because holiness and righteousness honor and glorify our great God.

Then there are convictions we hold simply because we are convicted to hold them. For example, I rarely if ever sit in the bar section of a restaurant. I don't like the ambiance, and in my opinion it is not a good testimony. Another example of my personal convictions has to do with Christians drinking alcoholic beverages. I don't believe a Christian should drink alcoholic beverages. It is a terrible testimony, and nothing good comes from it. I spent over twenty years in the navy, and I saw what alcohol does to a person's life. I could give you many other illustrations of my personal convictions, but they are mine and not binding on anyone else. The point here is simply that our convictions should come from God's Word. The apostle Paul said, "All things are lawful for me, but all things are not expedient: all things are lawful for me, but all things edify not" (1 Cor. 10:23). That means there are activities I might engage in as a Christian, but they do not build me up in my followership of Christ. Some activities have no specific biblical prohibition, but those activities do not edify me or anyone else. Therefore, I choose to bring my liberty in Christ under subjection to that which is beneficial for me and others I serve and minister to.

The third thing Paul said is that God's Word is good for reproof, which means correction. The moral compass of humans is broken by reason of our sin nature we inherited from Adam. Man is inherently on the wrong course in this life. Like a ship whose heading is off course, humans are headed down the path of sin and need a course correction. Jesus referred to the way of sin as being the broad way that leads to destruction. Jesus further revealed how there are many in the world who are taking the broad way of sin. Jesus called those who would follow Him to enter at the strait gate and thus walk the narrow way of moral righteousness and obedience. Furthermore, in relation to the broad way and those who travel that path, those who enter the strait gate and walk the narrow way are relatively few (Matt. 7:13). God's Word is the only source by which a human's moral path can be corrected. Accordingly, God's Word is the only instrument whereby humans are convicted of their sin and drawn to humble repentance and saving faith in Jesus Christ. The apostle Paul said, "For I am not ashamed of the gospel of Christ: for it is the power of God unto salvation to everyone that believeth; to the Jew first, and also to the Greek" (Rom. 1:16). The gospel message has the power to convict the sinner and draw him or her to saving faith and a spiritual new birth. No other message has that kind of power.

The Word of God is not only profitable for calling sinners to repentance but for instructing those who are saved in how to walk the path of holiness. Even after we are saved, it is easy to drift or get off course. The flesh is weak, and without constant course correction by way of God's Word as applied by the Holy Spirit, it is easy to slip back into the sin of the flesh. To be a true follower of Christ requires constant and vigilant attention to the choices one makes in life. God's Word serves as a constant light to our feet for making the necessary corrections that keep us on course. The true follower of Jesus should regularly check the course of his or her life against the perfect compass of God's Word.

Fourth, Paul said the Word of God is good for correction. The Greek word for correction is *epanorthosis*, which means to correct or set right again. Reproof in the last paragraph speaks of correction as a call from error. The idea here adds to the last in that the corrected person is set right before God. The Word of God is profitable for calling sinners out of sin and into a restored and right relationship with Him. Furthermore, the word can be applied to those who are saved when we are corrected from our carnality to a pure and holy walk with the Lord. To be a disciple of Christ one must be willing to be corrected by the Word of God. There are some who claim to be followers of Jesus, but they are not willing to be set right; their hearts are not open to be instructed by God's Word. A true follower of Jesus must be teachable and thus correctable. There is no spiritual growth unless we are teachable.

I was visiting in the home of a man once whose life was a mess. He was plagued with a myriad of physical ailments because of his heavy addiction to alcoholic beverages. In addition to his physical sufferings, he was divorced, his grown children were in all sorts of trouble, and he was living with a girlfriend who was just one in a long line of temporary companions. As I shared with this man, I reminded him of God's love, and I pleaded with him to turn from his sin and trust God by faith unto forgiveness. The man told me he was familiar with what the Bible says about God's love and the penalty of sin; he had attended church regularly when he was younger. The man told me he liked his drinking and his women, so he would not be repenting and giving them up anytime soon. This man refused to be corrected by God's Word. A few years later I preached his funeral. There was not much I could say concerning his soul. I used the opportunity to reach out to others who ran in his circle, warning them to hear God's Word while they could. One of the greatest dangers in life is to be unteachable.

Finally, Paul tells us that God's Word is profitable for instruction in righteousness. Earlier we understood that new believers in Christ are like newborn babies. They start out on the milk of the Word, and as they grow, they advance to eating more solid and substantial foods. Just like children who learn and grow physically, the child of God grows and learns by way of the inspired Word of God. Christian education is vital to true biblical followership of Christ. When Jesus gave the great commission, He said, "Go ye therefore, and teach all nations, baptizing them in the name of the Father, and of the Son, and of the Holy Ghost: Teaching them to observe all things whatsoever I have commanded you" (Matt. 28:19–20a). The church is specifically tasked by Jesus with teaching the Word of God. It has been astutely observed that biblical instruction is vital for both the mental and moral development of a Christian.[13] A follower of Christ is instructed in righteousness by the Word of God. As we learn God's Word

---

[13] Charles Tidwell, *The Educational Ministry of a Church.* (Nashville, TN: Broadman & Holman, 1996), 1.

and commit it to our heads and our hearts, it is God the Holy Spirit who empowers us to walk in the way we have learned.

The need for instruction in righteousness should be self-evident in our own lives. Like the apostle Paul, we desire to do what pleases God but often find ourselves doing the exact opposite of what we know is right. Then there are the sins of omission when we know what we are supposed to do and yet fail to act. Regular instruction in God's Word helps us be faithful and consistent followers of Christ. Instruction in God's Word does not happen by accident; it requires self-discipline. Mental and moral education requires personal effort. The apostle Paul said to Timothy, "Study to shew thyself approved unto God, a workman that needeth not to be ashamed, rightly dividing the word of truth" (2 Tim. 2:15). This admonition clearly applies to preachers, such as Timothy; however, it applies to all followers of Christ who desire to truly emulate their Lord. God's inspired Word is the standard by which we measure our progress in the Christian life. The inspired Word of God is the standard by which we measure our apprenticeship as followers of Christ. We need instruction in righteousness, and God's Word is the only resource by which that can happen.

One of the programs our church employs to teach God's Word to our children is the AWANA program (Approved Workmen Are Not Ashamed) as taken from 2 Tim. 2:15. This program is designed to teach the Bible to our children through verse memorization, biblical teaching, missionary studies, and recreational fun. A child who enters this program at a kindergarten age will graduate from the program when he or she enters the seventh grade having memorized over five hundred Bible verses. The young teenager then enters our youth program, where they continue to receive dedicated instruction in God's Word.

Instruction in God's Word is just as important for our adults. I purposely preach three times a week, teaching the Bible through expositional messages that explain what a passage means and how it can be applied to our lives in the twenty-first century. We have weekly small group Bible studies for every age. Special Bible studies are scheduled throughout the year to deal with specific biblical topics. One of the primary functions of the local church body is to teach and educate Christians in God's Word. There is no way to call Christians to be followers of Christ if we are not teaching them God's Word.

Since God's Word is so vital to our followership of Christ, perhaps we should each evaluate our personal habits as pertains to reading and studying the Bible. The true believer in Christ should read the Bible every day. Just as we eat food every day, just as yesterday's meal will not suffice for today's hunger, so we should not rely on yesterday's reading to carry us spiritually through the day today. Daily reading and meditation upon the Word of God is the instrument by which the indwelling Holy Spirit teaches us and draws us closer to the likeness of Jesus. There should be a certain hunger in the heart of the child of God to know Him more and more. The only way that hunger can be satisfied is by consuming God's Word.

Another important aspect of being instructed in God's Word comes by way of corporate worship and preaching. Placing ourselves under the influence of preaching and teaching is an essential aspect of Christian growth that should not be ignored. Attending church regularly and participating in Bible study groups is tremendously helpful in our desire to grow spiritually. The apostle Paul said God has given gifted men to the church—those who are called and gifted of God to preach, teach, and make clear the things God would have us know (Eph. 4:7–12). One of the evidences of a genuine follower of Christ is a hunger to be where God's Word is clearly expounded for the learning and edification of all. Those who would be growing followers of Christ must make use of God's Word, which is an indispensable part of the process. Just as there is no physical growth without food, there is no spiritual growth as a follower of Christ without reading and learning God's Word.

Active Prayer Life

Sustaining spiritual growth and an ever-increasing conformity to the image of Christ is not only dependent on the spiritual nourishment we gain from the Word of God; it is also dependent on an active and vital prayer life. Prayer is not an optional Christian exercise that we can treat as a take-it-or-leave-it endeavor; it is a natural and normal part of walking with Jesus. We cannot be genuine followers of Christ if we neglect prayer. Prayer is having a conversation with God. In Jesus Christ, we have the right to take our petitions to the very throne room of heaven. We can enter the presence of God Almighty twenty-four hours a day, seven days a week. To illustrate the importance of prayer, we might use our relationship with our spouse. My wife would not like it if I never talked to her. Because I love her, and we have a sweet relationship, I talk and commune with her all the time. Likewise, how can we have ongoing fellowship with God if we never talk with Him? If we love God and desire to walk with Him, prayer should be a regular part of our life. Jesus gave His disciples specific instruction concerning how we should pray.

> But when ye pray, use not vain repetitions, as the heathen do: for they think that they shall be heard for their much speaking. Be not ye therefore like unto them: for your Father knoweth what things ye have need of, before ye ask him. After this manner therefore pray ye: Our Father which art in heaven, Hallowed be thy name. Thy kingdom come. Thy will be done in earth, as it is in heaven. Give us this day our daily bread. And forgive us our debts, as we forgive our debtors. And lead us not into temptation but deliver us from evil: For thine is the kingdom, and the power, and the glory, forever. Amen. (Matt. 6:7–13)

Jesus gave this prayer as an example—a model of how we are to approach the Father. Jesus did not give us this prayer to be repeated as some formal petition we are to offer up when the occasion calls for it. There is nothing inherently wrong with using this prayer; however, Jesus gave the prayer primarily as an example for us to follow. Let's consider the parts of this prayer and what they mean to us as followers of Christ.

Jesus began His instruction by saying, "when ye pray." Jesus spoke in terms of an expectation; He took it for granted that we would pray. In other words, Jesus treated it as a natural habit of life that His followers would exercise an active prayer life. Jesus did not say *if* we pray, or when we feel like praying, He clearly speaks of prayer as a normal habit of one who is saved by faith—one who is His follower. Jesus is the ultimate example of what it means to have a prayer life. Jesus was continually in communion with the Father through prayer. It is often revealed in the gospels how Jesus set Himself apart from the crowds and ministry to spend time alone with the Father in prayer. We would do well in our Christian life to emulate Jesus in the matter of personal prayer.

Prayer is an essential part of spiritual growth, particularly when it is coupled with the reading, studying, and learning of God's Word. It has often been the case in my personal life that when I am engaged by the Word of God, I am moved to prayer. How natural it is for the child of God to read a passage of scripture, have it applied to his or her heart by the Holy Spirit, and then be moved to praise God for His marvelous love, grace, and mercy. On other occasions the Holy Spirit might so illuminate my understanding of a passage that I am left in awe of God's wisdom, glory, and majesty. In either case, I am moved to pray and have communion with such a great and awesome God.

The second thing Jesus pointed out in His model prayer has to do with the nature of prayer. The Pharisees had turned prayer into a public display. They prayed out loud in long phrases that were often repeated for effect. They stood on the street corner and prayed out loud, so people could both see and hear them. They were praying for show—praying to impress people. The Pharisees' goal in prayer was to impress others and put on a display of what they thought was religious righteousness. These false religious leaders wanted to impress people and receive the admiration of those who watched and listened to them. Jesus commanded His disciples to avoid such vain or empty repetitions, which have no value. Jesus taught that prayer is not for public display but rather is an intimate conversation with our heavenly Father. Public prayer is often part of our public worship together, and there is nothing wrong with praying out loud. However, the one praying audibly should remember that prayer is a sweet communion with our heavenly Father and should be offered with genuine humility apart from all hypocrisy. We do not pray or engage in any other form of public worship to impress people or to receive their admiration. Prayer is talking to God, even if others have the privilege to listen in. Emphasis is added to the point when Jesus said that our heavenly Father knows what we have need of before we ask Him. In other words, we do not have to convince God of our need with fancy prayers or petitions; He already knows.

Most of my life I have attended churches where the offering is received as part of the worship service. It is common practice that one of the ushers prays over the offering before the plates are passed throughout the congregation. There have been times when it seems the man chosen to pray takes the opportunity of public prayer to catch up on his prayer life! He prays for everyone and everything he can think of. Furthermore, it is amazing that when some people pray publicly, they speak to God with a different vocabulary—words they would never use in normal conversation. We are not to pray with these ostentatious displays of religiousness. Prayer is a conversation with our heavenly Father, not a religious exercise to impress others.

Jesus began His instruction concerning prayer by telling us how to address God. He said, "Our Father which art in heaven, Hallowed be thy name" (Matt. 6:9). It is important to understand that only those who are the redeemed of Christ have the right to approach God in this way. The Old Testament saint had no right to petition God as Father. Those who are lost in their sin have no right to address God as Father. It is often presumed that all human beings are children of God simply because God is our creator. The truth, however, is only those who are saved by faith in Jesus—those who are spiritually born into the family of God—have the incredible privilege to call God our Father. When the children of God pray, we can address Him as Father.

A second element of addressing God in prayer has to do with reverence and praise for who He is. God's name is holy because it represents His holy and perfect nature. Part of our communication with God should be filled with offerings of praise for who He is and what He has done for us. God's grace and mercy endures forever; so should our praise and adoration. Before we bring our petitions before the Father, may we bring our praise for who He is. God's name is often defamed and blasphemed by the world; we should do all in our power to address Him with the utmost respect and honor. Furthermore, the habit of our lives should be such as brings honor and glory to Him. Jesus said we should begin our prayer with praise and reverence to our great God who loves us and has saved us.

The next element of Jesus's model prayer has to do with surrendering our will to the will of the Father. Jesus said, "Thy kingdom come. Thy will be done in earth, as it is in heaven" (Matt. 6:10). It is appropriate in our prayers to ask for God's kingdom to come. God's will is inextricably connected to His kingdom. In asking for His kingdom to come, we express our inherent desire to see the kingdom of God expand on earth through the evangelistic efforts of the church. Furthermore, we desire to see the return of Christ to establish His promised kingdom on earth. The lost world is in a state of complete rebellion against God and His kingdom. As the redeemed of Christ, we genuinely desire and petition for the kingdom of God to be expressed in this world. When Jesus brings in His kingdom, wickedness and rebellion will be abolished. God's will is perfectly expressed in heaven. As the redeemed of Christ, we desire for God's will to be likewise fully expressed on the earth. When Jesus returns, evil and wickedness will be eradicated while holiness and righteousness will rule the day.

In light of Jesus's instruction to pray for God's will on this earth and thus the arrival of His kingdom, one might ask what has happened to the contemporary church of our day. It seems many who profess to be followers of Christ live from a decidedly secular worldview. In other words, many professed followers of Jesus seem to live for the here and now. In many Christian circles there is no focus on expanding the kingdom of God in this world through the proclamation of the gospel; nor is there a genuine desire for the return of Christ. I suspect there will be many professing Christians caught by surprise when Jesus raptures His church from this world. Sadly, there will be many professing Christians who are left here when Jesus calls His church out of this world—left here because they were never really followers of Christ in the first place.

Jesus warned that there will be those who are not ready when He returns. In Matthew 25 Jesus told the parable of the ten virgins. These ten virgins were waiting for the arrival of the bridegroom. They knew he was to arrive soon, but they did not know the exact time. Five of the virgins brought their lamps but no extra oil; the Bible calls them foolish. The other five brought their lamps along with some extra oil; the Bible calls these five virgins wise. When the bridegroom tarried long, the lamps began to run low on oil. The five with no oil had to leave and go in search of more oil. The five who were prepared simply refilled their lamps and continued to wait. The bridegroom came at midnight, and the five wise virgins went in and enjoyed the wedding feast. The five foolish virgins returned later and were not permitted to enter after the wedding had begun. When the five foolish virgins asked to enter, the Lord said, "Verily, I say unto you, I know you not" (Matt. 25:12b). They were not ready.

What do we learn from this parable? The clear lesson is that not everyone who claims the name of Jesus will be ready to enter the kingdom when it comes. I would suggest there are many today who are not ready for Jesus to return. The model prayer of our Lord teaches us to pray for His kingdom. If we claim the name of Jesus let us desire what the Father desires. If we claim to be part of the family of God, let us love what God loves, hate what God hates, and daily pray for God's will in the world around us. We can be an expression of the will of God in the world when the will of God for our lives is the priority position from which we live.

Jesus then showed us that it is completely appropriate to ask our heavenly Father for the things we need in this life. Jesus said, "Give us this day our daily bread" (Matt. 6:11a). There are necessities of life that enable us to live and serve God. We have physical necessities such as food, shelter, and clothing. We have interpersonal needs such as friends, family, and companionship. God is the source from which all our needs are met. We do well to notice there is a humble satisfaction in this request for provisions. The idea of daily provisions speaks of confidence in God's care for our daily needs. There is no idea here of great wealth—storehouses of provisions, grandiose houses, or even closets full of clothes and shoes. The humble request, presented with the utmost confidence and faith, is that God the Father will meet our needs as they arise. God meets our needs because He loves us, and so we may be faithful to do the work He has called us to do.

The health, wealth, and fame gospel we hear and see so prevalent in the Western culture of our day is in sharp contrast to what we find in God's Word. There is no promise in the Bible that a follower of Christ will enjoy perpetual health, large bank accounts, or even fame in this world. Contrary to that line of thinking and teaching, the Bible says, "Yea, and all that will live godly in Christ Jesus shall suffer persecution" (2 Tim. 3:12). The fact is, the more we look like Jesus in this world, the more the world will hate and persecute us. The degree to which God blesses us with this world's possessions is completely up to Him. Those whom God blesses with the wealth of this world will be held accountable for how they use it in the kingdom's work. God never blesses us with excess material possessions to be used exclusively in the satisfying of our fleshly lusts in the pleasures and things of this world. Jesus said we are to pray for our daily provisions and thus be content with God's provision in our lives. Every true follower of Jesus should keep in mind that we are responsible before God for our stewardship of all God blesses us with in this life, including our material possessions.

In the model prayer Jesus set before us we also find His instruction to confess our sin. Even after we are saved, we struggle with sin daily. As soon as we sin or fail God in some way, we are to confess that sin immediately. Keeping a short account of sin enables unbroken fellowship with the Father and a life marked by the fruit of the Spirit. Furthermore, we are to forgive others in the same way God forgives us. We cannot expect God's gracious forgiveness of our sin if we harbor hatred and unforgiveness for the deeds of others.

Confession of sin by the person who is already saved does not mean he or she is being saved all over again. Some equate confession of sin as being singularly practiced in the salvation event. However, the confession of sin continues in our lives even after we are saved. The difference is that confession of sin after we are saved has nothing to do with redemption; rather it has to do with sanctification. In other words, salvation is a one-time event that can never be repeated. Those who have been genuinely saved by faith in Jesus are forever saved—they can never be lost again. There is no need to pray for salvation over and over, for there is true security for the child of God. Jesus assured us of salvation's permanence when He said, "My sheep hear my voice, and I know them, and they follow me: And I give unto them eternal life; and they shall never perish, neither shall any man pluck them out of my hand" (John 10:27–28). Jesus said His redeemed will never perish, which means we can never be lost once we are saved by faith in Him. What we discover, however, is that after we are saved by faith in Jesus, we begin a lifelong sanctification process whereby the Holy Spirit is at work in us conforming us to the image of Christ. It does not take long after we are saved to realize we still struggle with sin. In other words, we still sin after we are saved. We do not sin because we desire to sin; we sin because our flesh is weak. It is difficult to make it through the day without thinking an errant thought, allowing our emotions to go unchecked, or failing to do what God has commanded us to do. Therefore, we pray for God's forgiveness, not to be resaved, but to maintain a close walk and fellowship with our Lord.

A good illustration is found in our own families. I have two sons and two daughters. My children are my children no matter what they might do. Their relationship to me as their father can never be undone. The moment they were birthed into our family, they were my children, permanently. The relationship I have with my children can never be changed; however, the choices they make in life can dramatically affect our fellowship. If one of my children decides to defy the rules of the home, our fellowship moves from one of joy and mutual encouragement to one of discipline and correction. In those times of discipline and correction, some of the joy is lost until there is repentance and restored obedience. Our children often think they are the only one's suffering pain when they are disciplined. But we know as parents there is pain and heartache in having to discipline them. Our relationship with God functions the same way. There is wonderful joy and encouragement when we walk with our Lord in obedience to His Word. However, in those times we choose to disobey, or we fall into sin unexpectedly, the remedy is immediate confession and repentance. The joy of our salvation and the encouragement of our walk with Jesus is maintained when we confess our sin. The apostle John said it this way: "If we say that we have no sin, we deceive ourselves, and the truth is not in us. If we confess our sins, he is faithful and just to forgive us our sins, and to cleanse us from all unrighteousness" (1 John 1:8–9). The apostle John wrote this statement concerning Christians, not lost people. Part of our prayer life should include the confession of all known sin.

Not only did Jesus instruct us to confess our sin; He instructed us to ask for deliverance from temptation. Jesus said, "And lead us not into temptation but deliver us from evil" (Matt. 6:13a). This is certainly a prayer we should be praying first thing in the morning every day. Why should we pray for deliverance from temptation? Because our flesh is weak, and we are no match for the wiles of the devil. Far better it is to be delivered from temptation itself than to struggle with the weakness of the flesh. It is by the power of the indwelling Holy Spirit that we have victory over sin. It is a worthy prayer that we seek God's deliverance from temptation, which leads to sin and failure. I say from the pulpit all the time that every born-again child of God should have a prayer time first thing in the morning, every day. It is true we can pray any time of the day; there is no specific instruction for us to pray in the morning. However, I would much rather ask God to deliver me from temptation and sin before I have to deal with it than to fail God in sin and then have to confess at the end of the day.

Since we are talking about temptation and sin, the question might be asked, where does temptation begin? James gives us the answer: "But every man is tempted, when he is drawn away of his own lust, and enticed. Then when lust hath conceived, it bringeth forth sin: and sin, when it is finished, bringeth forth death" (James 1:14–15). The origin of sin is found within us. The ever-burning pilot light of lust and self-centered rebellion within us needs only the slightest breeze of temptation to be fanned into a raging flame. It is a relatively easy thing for Satan to tempt us to sin, for the latent seed of sin resides always in our fallen flesh. Our prayer of deliverance from temptation is a prayer that God will deliver us from our own propensity to embrace sin. We need God's power to resist temptation and sin. May we begin each new day asking for that power.

Fellowship

So far, we have seen that spiritual growth is connected to spiritual nourishment in God's Word, exercised in an active prayer life. A third element we find essential to Christian spiritual growth is active involvement in a local body of believers—a local church. When we talk about involvement in a local church, we are talking about involvement in a local congregation that reflects the biblical idea of the universal church of Jesus Christ. It has been astutely observed that false churches have been a problem in Christianity from the beginning.[14] What then separates a true church from a false church? How can we tell the difference? According to Charles Tidwell, the meaning of a true church of Jesus Christ begins with the word *ekklesia*.[15] Ekklesia means those who are called out; it refers to an assembly of chosen people. The true church is therefore composed of those who are the called of Christ—the redeemed of Christ—those who have been saved by faith in Him. The church assembly is thus characterized by a gathering of

---

[14] Avery Dulles, *Models of The Church.* (New York: Image Books, 2002), 115.

[15] Tidwell, *The Educational Ministry of a Church,* 46.

the redeemed of Christ. Church membership as an administrative practice does not mean a person is saved and thus an actual member of the true church. A person may walk forward or raise his or her hand or fill out a card, but that does not make that person saved, nor does it make them a part of the true church of Jesus Christ. Participation in the true church of Jesus means a person is saved by faith and thus moved by the Holy Spirit to take part in the fellowship of the saints in a local gathering. Spiritual growth for the child of God is, to a large part, dependent upon active fellowship in a local church body. There is no such thing as a lone ranger Christian—all who are saved are part of the universal body of Christ.

What is it about a local body of believers—a gathering of those who are the redeemed of Christ—that facilitates the spiritual growth of individual believers? We find the answer to this question in the letter to the Hebrews: "And let us consider one another to provoke unto love and to good works: Not forsaking the assembling of ourselves together, as the manner of some is; but exhorting one another: and so much the more, as ye see the day approaching" (Heb. 10:24–25). There are four spiritually beneficial admonitions in this passage that directly apply to spiritual growth. We are to consider one another, provoke one another to love and good works, be faithful to the assembling together of the church, and continually be involved in exhorting one another. Let's consider what these four elements mean for our spiritual growth.

The first thing the writer to the Hebrews said is that we are to consider one another in the local fellowship of believers. The word *consider* comes from the Greek word *katanoeo*, which means to observe intently and consider what is observed. One writer from the early twentieth century described this kind of consideration as a "mutual regard," an exercising of kind consideration for one another in every area of Christian walk and personal need.[16] In the Christian fellowship of the church there is a mutual care for one another. Those who are saved by faith in Jesus have a spiritual familial relationship; we are the children of God and therefore spiritual brothers and sisters in Christ. Within the fellowship of the church we minister to one another's needs. If we see a fellow brother or sister in Christ who is walking through a rough experience in life, we consider their situation with compassion, care, and ministry as needed and as is

---

16 H. D. M. Spence-Jones, ed., *Hebrews: The Pulpit Commentary*. (London; New York: Funk & Wagnalls, 1909), 262.

appropriate. Our consideration of one another includes accountability as well. If we see a brother in Christ who has been overcome by some open and evident sin, we prayerfully come alongside him and lovingly encourage him to repent of sin and obey God. There is a mutual accountability in that we encourage one another to holiness and obedience to God's Word. The people we spend the most time with are the people who exercise the greatest amount of influence on our lives, particularly in the area of our conduct. I enjoy fellowship with those who love Jesus and demonstrate that love by way of an obedient lifestyle. They are the people I want to surround myself with because they are the people that I want influencing my life.

When we consider one another in the body of Christ it also includes the practice of mentorship. New believers in Christ need mentorship; they need training; they need someone to help them learn to follow Jesus. New believers in Christ benefit greatly from the influence of spiritually mature believers who can provide help and encouragement in their new walk with the Lord. We have already seen that a new believer in Christ is a spiritual baby who begins on the milk of the Word (1 Pet. 2:2). A more mature Christian mentor can help explain the Bible while teaching and demonstrating practical application in life. A new Christian can in essence watch a mature Christian and learn of the Christian life. For example, a new brother in Christ learns how to be a godly man by reading the Bible and interacting with other godly men. Mature Christians can serve as a model or prototype for baby Christians to follow.

My four children are an example of how we influence lifestyle. None of my children have ever woke up on Sunday morning and asked me if we were going to church. From the time they were babies we attended church as a family. They each began in the nursery, moved to the preschool department, were promoted to the children's department, participated in the youth department, and eventually graduated high school and became young adults. The pattern and influence upon their lives has always been that of corporate worship and faithfulness to our God. They learned from the earliest age that our family would be in church on Sunday morning, and they never asked me otherwise. My oldest two children are now grown and can make their own decisions concerning God and their faithfulness to corporate worship. As adults they both choose to serve God and be faithful to His church. That is how our Christian influence works in the body of Christ.

Not only do we consider one another in the body of Christ; we provoke one another as well. The writer to the Hebrews said we are to provoke one another to love and good works. The idea of being provoked or experiencing provocation is almost always expressed in negative terms. For instance, we are all familiar with being provoked to anger by some form of irritation. A driver, for example, who is inconsiderate and aggressive can provoke us to anger or at a minimum to ill feelings toward them. However, the general idea behind the word provoke is to stimulate a reaction. The Bible teaches us that it is possible to have positive spiritual stimulation in our lives. In fact, positive spiritual stimulation will enhance positive personal spiritual growth.

The first provocation or stimulation we are to exercise in the church is unto love. We are to interact in such a way that God's love is stimulated in our lives. Love is the highest expression of the Christian life, for it is the ultimate expression of God in us. The Bible declares that God is love (1 John 4:8). It stands to reason, therefore, that if we are living a fully surrendered life in the power of the Holy Spirit, the first outward evidence of God in our lives should be love. God's love is not some sentimental emotion that makes us feel all mushy inside. God's love is a cognitive-determined disposition that is not based on the worth or value of the one being loved. In other words, God chooses to love us even though we do not deserve to be loved. We have nothing of value to offer God, and yet He chooses to love us anyway. That is the kind of love we are to provoke in one another. Within the family of God, we are to love one another as God has loved us, and that means unconditionally. As we experience unconditional love in the church, we are provoked to do the same outside the church.

Jesus had a lot to say about love. For example, He said we are to love God with our whole being—all that we are: "Thou shalt love the Lord thy God with all thy heart, and with all thy soul, and with all thy mind. This is the first and great commandment. And the second is like unto it, thou shalt love thy neighbour as thyself" (Matt. 22:37–39). Fellowship in the body of believers provokes us and stirs us up to this kind of love. Followers of Jesus who forsake the assembly of believers can easily grow cold in their love for God, the church, and the lost world as well.

Many years ago, I was aware of a preacher who lived and served in the community where I then lived. One day his teenage daughter was at the shopping mall with her friend. They decided to split up, as the pastor's daughter had decided to go home. The pastor's daughter never made it home, and the police soon became involved. An investigation revealed the pastor's daughter had been abducted in the parking lot as she tried to enter her car. She was sexually assaulted and murdered. Law enforcement later found her body and notified the preacher and his wife of the terrible news. Within hours the police had a suspect, and he was arrested within a day or so of the crime. The evidence showed beyond a shadow of a doubt that the police had the right man; he would go on trial for murder in the first degree. As the suspected killer waited in jail for his day in court, the preacher requested that he be allowed to meet with the man who had taken his daughter from him. The meeting was approved by the sheriff, and with supervision the preacher met with the man who was accused of murdering his daughter. The preacher told the young man that he had done a terrible thing—he had taken the life of an innocent young lady. The preacher then told the young man that God loved him and wanted to save his soul. The preacher went on to share the gospel with this man who had just days before murdered his daughter. We instinctively ask, How could he do that? How could he care about the soul of the man who murdered his daughter? The answer is found in the unconditional love of Jesus Christ. Jesus loves us no matter what we have done. We are provoked to this same kind of love through the fellowship of the church. The preacher loved this man in Jesus, not for what he had done but because Jesus loved him despite what he had done.

The second provocation we experience in the body of Christ is unto good works. I was asked not long ago by a church member to define good works from a biblical perspective. What are good works in the Christian life? Good works are "works that are pure as to their motive, lawful as to their execution, and God-glorifying as to their aim."[17] A pure, lawful, and God-glorifying life is exactly what the true follower in Jesus is called to. Concerning the specifics of good works, Jesus said, "Let your light so shine before men, that they may see your good works, and glorify your Father which is in heaven" (Matt. 5:16). There is no all-encompassing list of good works; however, I believe we can put Christian good works in two broad categories. First, there are those good works associated with taking the gospel to the world. Sharing the gospel with a lost person is a good work—perhaps one of the greatest.

---

[17] Alan Cairns, *Dictionary of Theological Terms* (Belfast; Greenville, SC: Ambassador Emerald International, 2002), 197.

The preacher sharing the gospel with the man who murdered his daughter is a good work. Teaching a small Bible study group is a good work. Serving and teaching children in vacation Bible school is a good work. Singing in the choir, visiting the sick, or encouraging those who are hurting are all good works that the world can see and that can serve as a reflection of our relationship with Jesus. The second category of good works fall under what I call our social ministry to others. Social ministries include good works such as helping the homeless, providing food for the hungry, working in a pregnancy crisis center, helping in disaster relief or any other ministry that expresses a God-given concern for others. It is through meeting the social needs of others that we are often provided opportunity to share the gospel and thus seek to meet the lost person's deepest spiritual need. A follower of Christ who is actively involved in a local church where good works are actively pursued will be provoked to participate in good works.

The third provocation is faithfulness to the local church and corporate worship. It is easy for the world to crowd in and rob us of our corporate worship time. It seems that contemporary society is full of sporting events, children's programs, recreational opportunities, and family plans, which all seem to draw us away from scheduled church gatherings. The writer to the Hebrews admonishes us to make corporate worship a priority of our lives. We are not to forsake the assembling together of the church body, as was already the custom of some in the first century church. Why should corporate worship be a priority? First, we are social creatures, created in the image of God, who is Himself a social being. God is a triune being, He is one God expressed in three distinct persons. The Trinity is made up of God the Father, God the Son, and God the Holy Spirit. All three persons of the Trinity are one God. In the Trinity there has always been and always will be perfect harmony. We are created in the image of God, and we naturally thrive on social interaction. The church is a place of spiritual family where we can engage in good societal fellowship. The fact is that we are heavily influenced by the people we associate with. The Christian life is emboldened and empowered by our association with other Christians. Conversely, if we associate predominately with a lost world, the influence of the world will be heavy upon our lives and certainly influence us negatively.

Another reason for corporate worship is God's worthiness. When we worship God, it is an expression of His personal immeasurable worth. The writer to the Hebrews said, "By him therefore let us offer the sacrifice of praise to God continually, that is, the fruit of our lips giving thanks to his name" (Heb. 13:15). Corporate worship is an expression of our collective offering of praise to God. There is no spiritual growth or maturity apart from praise and worship of our great God. The redeemed of Christ are members of a spiritual family. We are never drawn closer to one another in that spiritual family than when we worship and praise God together. The admonition is that we forsake not the assembling of the saints in the local church body. We must be careful to not allow the busyness and temporal entrapments of this world to rob us of the sweet fellowship of the local church body. Spiritual growth is inextricably connected to corporate fellowship and worship.

Finally, the writer to the Hebrews instructs us to exhort one another in the faith. Corporate worship lends itself to the Christian function of exhortation. The Greek word for exhortation is *parakaleo*. The basic meaning of the word includes help, comfort, aid, encouragement, and a call to carry on—keep going. Given the context of corporate assembly, one writer said the word implies urgency in continuing in the faith.[18] It is in the context of the local church assembly that we find encouragement to continue when life is challenging. It is through the challenging times of life that we grow the deepest in our faith. It is quite natural for the flesh to become discouraged from time to time. Even the strongest of Christians can experience doubts if they are on a spiritual island, and the storm is raging all around them. John the Baptist had his time of doubt and weakness when he was in prison. "And John calling unto him two of his disciples sent them to Jesus, saying, Art thou he that should come? or look we for another?" (Luke 7:19). The suffering of prison life coupled with the prospect of being executed at any moment had caused John to rethink all he had professed and believed. Jesus's answer to John: "Go your way, and tell John what things ye have seen and heard; how that the blind see, the lame walk, the lepers are cleansed, the deaf hear, the dead are raised, to the poor the gospel is preached. And blessed is he, whosoever shall not be offended in me" (Luke 7:22–23). Jesus exhorted John to keep the faith and not be offended in Him. The same kind of exhortation takes place in the local assembly of the body of Christ. Our spiritual growth is enhanced when we are exhorted by others to keep the faith.

---

[18] David Allen, *Hebrews: The New American Commentary.* (Nashville, TN: B&H Publishing, 2010), 519.

Service

A growing follower of Christ not only needs spiritual nourishment through the Word of God, an active prayer life, and regular fellowship in the body of the local church; the person needs an outlet where spiritual gifts and abilities can be exercised for the edification of others. The Bible tells us that every born-again child of God is given specific grace by God to serve in the body of believers. The apostle Paul said, "But unto every one of us is given grace according to the measure of the gift of Christ" (Eph. 4:7). Paul specifically said, "every one of us." The universality of spiritual gifts inherently means we are all expected to participate in the ministry of the local church body. The is no hierarchy in the church where certain people have all the spiritual gifts and abilities to serve while everyone else just sits around doing nothing. Every true child of God possesses spiritual gifts and abilities that should be used to contribute to the ministry of the church. Not only do we possess these spiritual gifts; we are expected by God to employ them for His glory and the benefit of the church.

Not only does every child of God have spiritual gifts and abilities to employ in the body of Christ; those gifts and abilities are as unique as the person upon whom they are bestowed. The God who created every person is the same God who graces each person with just the right spiritual gifts and abilities to fit his or her individual personality and demeanor. Just as each child of God is uniquely made, so the spiritual gifts and abilities are uniquely given. Because the child of God is uniquely created and gifted by God, each person's ability to contribute to the work of the kingdom of God is unique and cannot be duplicated by another. Therefore, it is easy to see how important it is that each of us serves to the full capacity of what God has equipped and enabled us to do.

Why did God give each of His redeemed a unique spiritual gift? The Bible tells us that our spiritual gifts are for edification—the building up of the body of Christ, the church. The apostle Paul said, "And he gave some, apostles; and some, prophets; and some, evangelists; and some, pastors and teachers; For the perfecting of the saints, for the work of the ministry, for the edifying of the body of Christ: Till we all come in the unity of the faith, and of the knowledge of the Son of God, unto a perfect man, unto the measure of the stature of the fulness of Christ" (Eph. 4:11–13).

The purpose of these spiritual gifts is the edification and equipping of the saints. Spiritually gifted saints are given, by God, to the church for the growth of all. The gift of apostleship refers to the twelve chosen by Jesus. There is no biblical support for apostolic succession; the twelve apostles chosen by Jesus were specifically gifted by Him to lay the foundation of the church (see Eph. 2:20). Prophets were gifted in foretelling and forthtelling. With the completion of the canon of scripture, there is no new revelation to be added to the Bible. Prophets today are those who forthtell or proclaim the revealed Word of God. Evangelists are those who are specially gifted and called by God to share the gospel. Sharing the gospel with a lost world is every Christian's job; however, there are those whom God has gifted to be especially good at it. Pastors and teachers are two functions of the same person or office. The pastor is called of God to oversee and shepherd the flock of God—the church. One of the requirements to serve as a pastor is that a person be "apt to teach" (1 Tim. 3:2). Part of the job of a shepherd is feeding the sheep. The pastor feeds the flock of God in spiritual terms through teaching the Word of God.

The purpose of employing our spiritual gifts in the body of Christ is to assist every saint of God in reaching spiritual maturity and usefulness for God's glory and expansion of His kingdom. God has so designed our spiritual gifts that two things happen when we serve. First, those employing their spiritual gift grow in their spiritual walk with the Lord and receive a blessing. Second, those being ministered to grow in their spiritual walk with the Lord and are blessed by the person ministering to them. Spiritual growth for the follower of Jesus is directly connected to serving Him in the local church body.

Summary

In this chapter, we learned that genuine believers in Jesus have a spiritual appetite. Just like eating food for our physical growth and health, the genuine follower of Jesus needs spiritual nourishment to remain spiritually healthy and to promote spiritual growth. Spiritual nourishment is found in God's Word—the Bible. Personal reading and meditation in God's Word are essential for spiritual vitality and a healthy spiritual immune system against sin. The corporate fellowship of the local congregation should be grounded in consistent teaching from God's Word. A church that majors on the Word of God will be spiritually healthy and productive.

Not only is the Word of God essential to spiritual growth and health; every follower of Christ should have an active prayer life. Prayer is a privilege of the redeemed to talk with God at any time. It is most difficult to experience spiritual growth if one never spends time in fellowship and communication with the heavenly Father. An active prayer life is essential to spiritual growth and effectiveness in service to the Lord.

Finally, fellowship and service in a local body of Christ is necessary for spiritual growth. All who are saved by faith in Jesus are part of His spiritual family. Christians need one another to grow in faith and spiritual maturity. Every child of God is given a spiritual gift to be employed in the church for the edification of all. Nowhere in the Bible do we find lone-ranger Christians who are just out there doing their own thing. Spiritual growth is always connected to participation in the corporate body of Christ. Are you a growing follower of Christ? If not, what is hindering you from being all God saved you to be?

Four
EFFECTIVENESS

S ome years back while serving as an officer in the navy, I assigned a young man to a painting job. His assignment for the day was to paint a passageway on the ship. Steel ships in saltwater create a perpetual state of corrosion, which means there is always a bulkhead, hatch, ladder, or handrail that needs sanding and a fresh coat of paint. I pointed out what I wanted the young man to do and left him to his work. A few hours later I went by the passageway to see how things were progressing. My expectation was that he had made considerable progress in making the passageway look new again. Much to my chagrin, I arrived at the passageway to discover the young man had barely progressed beyond the corner of the bulkhead where he started. Not hiding my agitation, I asked the young sailor what he had been doing for the last several hours. With complete sincerity and genuine shock at my displeasure, he reported that he had been painting the entire time. The young man in the story was painting, but he certainly was not an effective painter! He was engaged in painting, but his effectiveness left a lot to be desired.

The same kind of ineffectiveness can plague us in the Christian life. Some years ago, an older couple came to me and said they wanted to join the church. I was delighted God had led them to make the decision to be an active part of our local congregation of believers. However, their follow-on statement caused me no small concern. Immediately after indicating their desire to join the church, they informed me they were retired and would not be serving in any capacity in the church. They just wanted to be a part of the church, attend the services at their discretion, and have no responsibility of any kind. Both the husband and wife professed to know

Jesus as their personal Lord and Savior. They were followers of Christ in that they were saved; however, it is safe to say they were not effective followers of Christ. It is possible to be genuinely saved and yet ineffective for the cause of Christ. It is possible to be saved and then sit out one's entire Christian life on the sideline. In this chapter, we will consider what it means to be an effective follower of Christ.

God's Definition of Effectiveness

If we were to take a survey and ask Christians what it means to be an effective Christian, we would receive nearly as many different answers as the number of people we ask. Effectiveness in Christian ministry is almost always measured by some human standard. The small group Bible teacher measures success by the number of people that attend his class. The preacher measures ministry effectiveness by how large the church is, buildings, ministries, and numbers who attend. I knew a preacher once who measured ministry effectiveness almost exclusively by the number of baptisms he recorded each year. The individual Christian might measure effectiveness by how well he or she lives out the Christian life in accord with some code of conduct or degree of service that person has set. Rather than measure success in the Christian life by some arbitrary human standard, let's examine what the Bible says about God's definition of effectiveness.

In the simplest terms, to be effective means to be successful in a specific purpose or function. Our purpose as a genuine follower of Christ is to bring honor and glory to our heavenly Father. God has a path for each of us to walk and a purpose for each of us to fulfill. We are each responsible to do what God has gifted and equipped us to do. Jesus said, "Let your light so shine before men that they may see your good works and glorify your Father which is in heaven" (Matt. 5:16). Our good works are the things we do for the glory of God. An effective Christian life can then be defined as habitual surrender to the power of the Holy Spirit whereby the Holy Spirit produces in us the good works that bring honor and glory to God the Father. Though it is the power of the Holy Spirit that produces good works in us, we are not without responsibility in the process. We must surrender our will to the will of the Father. We must surrender ourselves to His purpose for our lives.

The apostle Peter helps us understand some of our responsibility when it comes to effective Christian living. Peter said, "And beside this, giving all diligence, add to your faith virtue; and to virtue knowledge; And to knowledge temperance; and to temperance patience; and to patience godliness; And to godliness brotherly kindness; and to brotherly kindness charity. For if these things be in you, and abound, they make you that ye shall neither be barren nor unfruitful in the knowledge of our Lord Jesus Christ" (2 Pet. 1:5–8). Peter specifically said that if we add these things to our faith, they will make us fruitful in the service of our Lord. The faith Peter speaks of here is saving faith. That means we are to add these things to our Christian life after we are saved so we might be fruitful—effective in the Christian life.

We begin our thoughts here with the realization that we must take an active role in adding these virtues to our lives. Effective Christian living does not happen by accident; we are not passive in the process. One writer has astutely observed that salvation is free by the will of God the Father, the finished work of Christ, and the calling of the Holy Spirit. But once we are saved, our walk with God becomes a "cost everything daily discipleship."[19] That is why Peter said, "give all diligence" (2 Pet. 1:5) in adding these virtues to our faith. Diligence is the Greek word *spoude*, which means to act with earnest zeal or genuine effort. Effective Christian living is not for the lazy or slothful of heart. We could be like the young sailor in my earlier illustration and stand in one corner of the Christian life, haphazardly doing what we perceive to be Christian activities, without ever really being effective for the Lord. We are to make a conscious decision to add these elements to our faith. There is no place for laziness in the effective Christian life. We have but one life to live for Jesus—one opportunity to make a difference in this world. A genuine follower of Christ is called to labor for the Master.

The first element of effectiveness in the Christian life is virtue or goodness. Virtue in and of itself means goodness. In the salvific context it means moral goodness before God—a life lived in willing conformity to God's law. A virtuous life is one that removes self from the throne and places Jesus on the throne. A virtuous life is one of practical surrender to

---

[19] Robert Utley, *The Gospel according to Peter: Mark and I & II Peter*, vol. 2, Study Guide Commentary Series (Marshall, TX: Bible Lessons International, 2000), 277.

the power of the Holy Spirit, so He might produce in us the fruit of the Sprit as spelled out in Galatians 5:22–23. As a pastor I have witnessed Christians struggle with the concept and practice of a virtuous life. The main reason they struggle is a lack of willing surrender to the will of God. In our flesh we are inherently self-centered. Our old sin nature desires to rule our lives—causes us to put self on the throne. The Holy Spirit will not rule over the life of one unwilling to offer it to Him. We must consciously and purposely say to the Lord, "your will and purpose for my life, not mine." The apostle Paul said we are to present our bodies a living sacrifice, holy and acceptable unto God, which is our reasonable service. He continued by saying we are to resist being conformed to this world by the transforming of our minds through the Word of God (Rom. 12:1–2). There is no practical goodness before God if we are allowing ourselves to be forced into the mold of this world. Christian virtue or goodness is produced in us by the Holy Spirit when we are willing for Him to do so.

I remember a time when my oldest daughter was playing with a stick and came away with a splinter in her finger. The splinter was painful, and she asked me if I could make it stop hurting. I told her I could remedy the whole situation, but that would require her allowing me to remove the splinter with a needle and tweezers. Her answer was slow in coming as she weighed the pain of the splinter against the pain of me digging it out of her finger. She finally decided it would be better to endure some pain now to make the whole thing go away. I removed the splinter and her finger healed quickly. That was only possible when she willingly presented her hand to me so I could remove the splinter. Our mortal life is full of all kinds of spiritual splinters, cuts, and bruises. We must surrender our lives to the Holy Spirit, so he can mend our wounds and heal our hurts.

To our virtue or goodness, we are to add an ever-increasing knowledge of God. We gain knowledge through two primary avenues—formal instruction and experience. It's best when we learn and gain knowledge through both instruction and experience at the same time. Academic instruction is always reinforced and strengthened by practical application. Our knowledge of God grows the same way. We grow in knowledge of God through the study of the Bible. The Word of God is the single infallible source from which we gain a more comprehensive knowledge of both the plan and character of God. God has fully revealed Himself in His Son Jesus Christ, and the Bible reveals all we need to know about Jesus. What we learn from the Bible is reinforced and strengthened by practical application in daily life. The more we walk with Jesus in the power of the Holy Spirit, the more we learn how to walk with Jesus in a way that honors Him. Every trial, tribulation, spiritual victory, and even our spiritual failures are lessons concerning the Christian life. We are to add to our faith a continuing knowledge of God, so we might be effective for Him in this life.

Then Peter said we are to add the virtue of temperance to our lives. Temperance is a word that means self-control. One writer said it is the, "restraint of the appetites and passions in accordance with reason."[20] The new convert in Christ discovers quickly that the flesh is still alive and active as an influence toward sin and disobedience. The apostle Paul admonished the believers in Ephesus to put off the old man and put on the new man, which is after God, "created in righteousness and true holiness" (Eph. 4:22–24). The simple truth is that we must exercise self-control and restraint when it comes to the passions of the flesh that draw us into sin and disobedience of God's Word. There can be very little effectiveness in the Christian life if we do not restrain the sinful appetites of the flesh. Such restraint requires a willingness on our part to surrender to the power of the Holy Spirit. The Spirit of God will never give us victory over sin that we are not willing to have victory over. Neither can we have practical victory over daily sin without the power of the Holy Spirit. We are called to resist sin and then rely on the power of the Holy Spirit to enable us to overcome sin.

Some years back I had a conversation with a man who was addicted to pornography. I shared the gospel with him and told him that Jesus would forgive all his sin and save his soul if he would confess with a repentant heart and ask. The man said he knew all about Jesus and the gospel. In fact, he told me he knew how to be saved. I then encouraged him to confess his sin to God and throw himself on God's mercy and grace. The man said he would not ask God to save him because he liked his sin and did not want to give it up. He told me he had no intention of living a pure life with his wife, and that was his decision. There is no deliverance from addiction for this man so long as he is unwilling to be delivered. The same is true of sin

---

[20] F. L. Cross and Elizabeth A. Livingstone, eds., *The Oxford Dictionary of the Christian Church* (Oxford, New York: Oxford University Press, 2005), 1594.

in the Christian life. Even after we are saved, we battle temptation and sin. We must be willing to confess and forsake our sin for God's power to be fully manifest in our lives.

To self-control, Peter said we are to add the virtue of patience. Biblical patience means endurance. It has often been said that the Christian life is not a sprint; it is a marathon. Effective Christian living is found in those who set their hearts to serve God for the long haul. I have seen Christians get on fire for God, and it is a wonderful thing to observe. However, some of them are like a shooting star; they serve God with great vigor for a season, and then they fade away and are never seen again. The Christians who are most effective for the cause of Christ in this world are those who continue to burn day in and day out; they endure the challenges of the Christian life and carry on. There are plenty of opportunities in the Christian life to just give up and go sit on the sidelines until Jesus either takes us home or raptures the church. There are many times in the service of our Lord where we may become discouraged and feel like giving up. But true effectiveness for God never quits and always endures as a good soldier of Christ.

I recently preached the funeral of a woman who was eighty-nine years old. I met her when she was seventy-four years old. She did more in the ministry of Jesus in the last fifteen years of her life than some Christians will do their entire lives. She worked in the children's ministry, was involved in small group Bible studies, and never failed to minister to other women in the church who were in need. Not only was she active in the church, she ministered to her husband of seventy-three years (she was married at age fifteen), and was a mother, grandmother, great-grandmother, and great-great-grandmother. This woman demonstrated genuine endurance as a child of God.

The next virtue Peter mentioned is godliness. The word means piety toward authority in one's life.[21] Respect for authority always begins with God. Piety is therefore most often associated with religious duty—the way one practices his or her faith in God. For the Christian, this means a reverential fear of God. The idea of fearing God in the Christian life is connected to respecting Him as our heavenly Father. The effective

---

[21] Peter H. Davids, *The Letters of 2 Peter and Jude*, The Pillar New Testament Commentary (Grand Rapids, MI: William B. Eerdmans, 2006), 181.

Christian life is one lived out in respect of God. We respect and reverence God because of His character, His perfect law, and His lordship in our lives. If we genuinely respect God, then we will be motivated to obey and serve God. If we genuinely reverence God, we will not want to offend Him by the choices we make in life. It's hard to believe a person respects God when the evidence of the person's lifestyle is that of perpetual disobedience to all God has called and commanded us to be.

After godliness, Peter said we are to add the virtue of brotherly kindness to our lives. Brotherly kindness speaks of our attitude toward others. Brotherly kindness is expressed toward fellow believers in Christ as well as the lost world. Those who are saved by faith in Jesus have been adopted into the family of God. Only saved people are truly the children of God. There is a fellowship among believers the world cannot know or understand. The apostle Paul said, "As we have therefore opportunity, let us do good unto all men, especially unto them who are of the household of faith" (Gal. 6:10). Peter said, "Finally, be ye all of one mind, having compassion one of another, love as brethren, be pitiful, be courteous" (1 Pet. 3:8). Brotherly kindness has a special reality within the family of God. This is another reason why it is completely out of character for a person to profess that he or she is a born-again child of God and yet have no desire to fellowship and serve alongside other believers in a local church congregation. The growing and effective Christian life will be marked by a passion and compassion for the family of God. The effective Christian will love the church as Jesus loves the church.

The virtue of brotherly kindness is also something we should express to all people. As the redeemed of Christ, we are to have compassion for the lost. Those who will live an effective and fruitful life in Christ will demonstrate a Christlike love for a lost world. Sharing the gospel with those around us while encouraging them to seek God in the day of opportunity are all part of brotherly kindness. If we are true followers of Christ, then we will interact with a lost world like He did. Jesus loves lost people and had compassion on them. After all, that is how you and I came to know him in the full pardon of our sin. Brotherly kindness will move us to show the love of Jesus to everyone with whom we come into contact.

The final virtue to be added to our faith is love. This should be no surprise, for love is the greatest of all the spiritual gifts. The apostle Paul said, "And now abideth faith, hope, charity, these three; but the greatest of these is charity" (1 Cor. 13:13). This love is not of the brotherly kind expressed in the previous virtue, but rather the Christlike love that caused Him to love us unconditionally. The Greek word is *agape*, which expresses the purest form of love. This love is free of emotional stimulus, free of selfish desire, free of ulterior motive, and is driven by conscious choice. In other words, *agape* love is a love of choice. God chose to love us, based on His own loving character, when we did not deserve to be loved. Likewise, we are called to love others, in the power of the Holy Spirit, regardless of whether we think or feel they deserve to be loved. We are to love others because God has first loved us. The effective Christian life will demonstrate unconditional love for others. This kind of love is not possible by human will. We do not have the capacity to love others unconditionally. Only the Holy Spirit can produce in us this kind of love for others.

How then might we define effective Christian living? In light of this passage, we could say that effective Christian living is that life that is surrendered to the will of God, empowered by the Holy Spirit, and is actively adding to saving faith the elements listed 2 Pet. 1:5–8. Notice that effective Christian living is not defined by many of the things perceived as success in contemporary Christian culture. The effective Christian is not necessarily the one who attends church all the time. Church attendance is an outflow of the effective Christian life; a growing effective Christian will want to be in church, but attendance itself does not make one effective. Furthermore, possessing and practicing some cultural, historical, or even pharisaical set of moral standards will not make nor constitute an effective Christian life. No, effective Christian living is measured by surrendering to God's will, living in the power of the Holy Spirit, and adding to our faith an ever-growing set of spiritual virtues.

Willing to Be A Servant

As previously noted, being a follower of Christ requires a willingness. Effective Christian living also requires a willingness. Effective Christian living is dependent upon our willingness to be a servant of the Lord. We find the example of willing servanthood in the life of the apostle Paul. Paul often referred to himself as the servant of the Lord. For example, Paul opened his letter to the church at Rome by saying, "Paul, a servant of Jesus Christ, called to be an apostle, separated unto the gospel of God" (Rom. 1:1). The word for servant in this verse is the Greek word *doulos*, which means a slave. The apostle Paul said he was a slave of Jesus Christ. What did Paul mean when he referred to himself as the slave of Christ? According to William Barclay, the word *doulos* carries several connotations. First, the word means to be "absolutely possessed by God." [22] Those who are saved by faith in Jesus have been redeemed—bought out of sin—by the blood of Jesus Christ. That means God owns us lock, stock, and barrel. To be owned by someone often carries a deservedly negative connotation. However, for the child of God there is nothing but benefit in the arrangement. God redeemed us from sin and made us His personal possession. It is an honor and privilege to be counted among those who belong to Christ. Paul was more than happy to identify himself as one possessed by God. The same privilege applies for us today.

Second, to be a slave, or *doulos*, of the Lord means to be completely at His disposal at all times and in all things. [23] The redeemed of Christ have no independent rights apart from the will of God for our lives. Since the redeemed of Christ are His personal possession, it easily follows that we are obligated to do all He commands. A faithful servant obeys the will of the Master. An effective follower of Christ will surrender self-control to the Holy Spirit in all areas of life. As a *doulos* we realize life is not about us. As a *doulos* we realize church is not about us. As a *doulos* we realize our temporal wants and wishes in this life are not the priority. An effective follower of Christ is one who is perpetually at His disposal to do that which pleases and brings honor and glory to Him.

Third, a *doulos* is characterized by "unquestioning obedience." [24] There may be times in the Christian life when God calls us to serve in places that are difficult, uncomfortable, unpleasant, or even dangerous or painful. Yet, as one who is owned by the Master, we have an obligation to go where He sends and do what He assigns. The prophet Isaiah stands as a wonderful example concerning unquestioning obedience. God said, "Whom shall I

---

[22] William Barclay, *The Letters of James and Peter*, 3rd ed., The New Daily Study Bible (Louisville, KY; London: Westminster John Knox Press, 2003), 337.

[23] Ibid, 338.

[24] Ibid.

send, and who will go for us?" (Isa. 6:8a). Isaiah responded, "Here am I; send me" (Isa. 6:8b). The principle of unquestioning obedience to the Lord seems to be a foreign concept in our contemporary Christian setting. In Christian circles today, it seems that far more emphasis is placed on what we want for ourselves than what God wants for us. In Christian circles today we seem to be far more enamored with what's in the Christian life for us here and now rather than focusing on doing what God has called us to do. An effective follower of Christ will simply obey.

Fourth, the concept of *doulos* means the redeemed of Christ are "constantly in the service of the Lord."[25] One of the things Christians often struggle with is the management of their time. As a pastor, I see men and women involved in all sorts of time-consuming activities in life. Some of these activities are necessary; for example, we must work and provide for our family's needs. However, it is easy to allow worldly endeavors to rob us of time that should be spent serving the Lord. The redeemed of Christ should make church attendance and participation in service to our God a top priority in life. When I say a top priority, I mean above all our recreational habits. There is nothing in this life that has more value than being available to do what God has called us to do.

We are all blessed with twenty-four hours in a day, 168 hours in a week. How are we investing those hours? As a *doulos* we are never off the clock in our service to the Lord. As the Master, God owns all our time. There is nothing wrong with taking a vacation; my family and I take one every year. There is nothing wrong with attending sporting events, participating in recreational events, and even enjoying hobbies. But be aware, those things can become disproportionate and hinder our service to the Lord. A man or woman can enjoy fishing or golf as a recreational event and perhaps as a means of relaxation. However, if he or she is fishing or golfing two or three days a week, that person's time management is out of balance. An effective follower of Christ is a willing servant of the Lord, all the time.

---

[25] Barclay, *The Letters of James and Peter*, 338.

Purity and Holiness

Purity and holiness seem to be lost concepts on our contemporary society. However, for the effective follower of Christ, these elements are essential and cannot be overlooked. Purity is often spoken of in the Bible regarding "guiltless, blameless, or innocent behavior."[26] The Lord Jesus Christ is the only one who can make a sinner guiltless or blameless before God the Father. Before we were saved by faith in Jesus, we were corrupt and utterly repulsive in the ugliness of our sin. Isaiah the prophet reminds us that the very best works we can produce in the flesh are no better than filthy rags (Isa. 64:6). Purity is only attainable by the cleansing power of the blood of Christ. By faith in Jesus He forgives our sin and places on us His purity—His righteousness. When God the Father looks at us, He sees the purity and righteousness of His Son.

When we talk about purity in the Christian life we are talking about purity in practical lifestyle. Purity in the New Testament focuses on moral purity, the integrity of one's life, the way we interact with other believers, and the moral boundaries we set for our lives.[27] The apostle Paul told Timothy that in a great house there are many kinds of vessels that might be used. Some of the vessels are of gold while others are of wood. Paul then went on to encourage Timothy to "purge" himself of sinful and unclean habits so he might be a "vessel unto honour, sanctified, and meet for the master's use, and prepared unto every good work" (1 Tim. 2:21). The message for us is clear; if we desire to be vessels fit for the Master's use, we must be diligent in pursuing pure lives in the power of the Holy Spirit. A child of God cannot live in open or unconfessed sin and then expect God to use him or her in the ministry for His honor and glory. An effective follower of Christ must be a pure follower of Christ—one who confesses sin as soon as it is known. The redeemed of Christ are called out of this world as it pertains to lifestyle. Purity should be the habit of our lives. Sin and impurity must be the exception to the rule.

Holiness is closely related to purity; that is why the two terms are often spoken of together. Holiness is a characteristic of the nature of God. In

---

[26] Walter Elwell, *Evangelical Dictionary of Biblical Theology*, Baker Reference Library (Grand Rapids: Baker Book House, 1996), 660.

[27] Ibid.

the same way that God is love (1 John 4:8), God is also holy (Rev. 4:8). God defines holiness by His very character—the infinite degree in which He is separate from everything else that exists. The first thought that comes to mind when one speaks of holiness is God.[28] God is the standard of holiness. God saved us to be conformed to the image of His Son, who being God, is holy. Therefore, God's eternal plan for His elect is that one day we will be perfectly holy in the likeness of Jesus. We are called to pursue holiness in this life, for it is our destiny in Jesus.

On the other end of the holiness spectrum is sinful man. "Holiness is not an intrinsic human quality."[29] The only way man becomes holy is by saving faith in Jesus Christ. At the moment of saving faith, Jesus forgives all our sin and then places on us His holiness, just as He placed on us His purity. We have a relationship and subsequently fellowship with God the Father because He sees us in His Son, Jesus Christ. It is in the holiness of Jesus that we are permitted to approach the throne of God in heaven. We have access to the Father through the Son.

The practical application is seen in the lifestyle of the child of God. Because we are positionally holy in Jesus Christ, we are called to live out that positional holiness in a practical daily lifestyle. God's holiness is marked by His separation from all that is less than perfectly holy. Our daily life should reflect an ongoing exercise of forsaking unholiness and pursuing all that is holy before our God. The apostle Paul said, "I beseech you therefore, brethren, by the mercies of God, that ye present your bodies a living sacrifice, holy, acceptable unto God, which is your reasonable service. And be not conformed to this world: but be ye transformed by the renewing of your mind, that ye may prove what is that good, and acceptable, and perfect, will of God" (Rom. 12:1–2). An effective follower of Christ is one who exercises purity and holiness as a habit of life—one who brings forth good works that honor God. This habit can only be formed in our lives as we consciously forsake sin and actively ask for God's power to embrace obedience and holiness.

---

[28] Carl Henry, *God, Revelation, and Authority* (Wheaton, IL: Crossway Books, 1999), 324.

[29] .

Power to Serve

One of the most interesting aspects of being an effective follower of Christ has to do with the power by which the ministry is accomplished. The ministry of the gospel is never effective based on the talents and abilities of the follower. All effective ministry must be performed in the power of the Holy Spirit, regardless of how talented, charismatic, or gifted the individual follower may be. God calls us to serve, God equips us to serve, and God empowers us to serve.

At the moment of salvation, the Holy Spirit bestows upon the believer at least one spiritual gift and often more than one. The apostle Paul spoke to the church in Rome concerning spiritual gifts when he said, "So we, being many, are one body in Christ, and everyone members one of another. Having then gifts differing according to the grace that is given to us" (Rom. 12:5–6a). We notice first how Paul identified our spiritual gifts as a grace of God. In other words, we do not determine what our spiritual gift is; God the Holy Spirit bestows on us the gift He wants us to have. We do not get to choose which spiritual gift we will have or exercise. This is particularly important to remember for those who might identify certain spiritual gifts as an evidence of true salvation. For example, there are some who hold that if a person does not have the gift of tongues, that person is somehow missing out on the full spiritual blessing of being saved. That is an errant doctrine, for we each have the spiritual gift or gifts God determined for us to have. We do not get to pick certain sign gifts just because we think they demonstrate more spirituality than some other gift, like teaching. I do not believe the sign gifts are active in the contemporary church today; however, if they were, we would not all be able to perform them. There would be some of us that the Holy Spirit did not grant those gifts to. God gave each of us the spiritual gifts he wanted each of us to have and employ in the local church for the edification of the whole body.

Next, we see how Paul employed the analogy of a body as concerns the diversity of our spiritual gifts. Paul used this same analogy when speaking to the church in Corinth. "For as the body is one, and hath many members, and all the members of that one body, being many, are one body: so also is Christ. For by one Spirit are we all baptized into one body, whether we be Jews or Gentiles, whether we be bond or free; and have been all made to drink into one Spirit. For the body is not one member, but many" (1 Cor. 12:12–14). The church is here likened to the human body. Just as the human body has many parts, each with its own individual function, so the body of Christ has many members, each with their own unique spiritual gift. Each part of the human body performs its individual function for the benefit of the whole body. The heart, for example, does one important thing that no other organ of the body can do; it pumps blood. The heart's unique function is carried out to the benefit of all the other organs and the body as a whole. Likewise, when we employ our individual spiritual gifts in the power of the Holy Spirit, the whole body of Christ—the church—is blessed.

I was reminded of the reality of this analogy a few years ago when I wrecked my motorcycle. I was in the mountains of North Carolina with some friends on a weeklong ride. I was in the back of the pack and came around a corner at nearly fifty miles per hour. They had all stopped to figure out how to get to the place we were headed. The problem is, they stopped in the middle of this country road. When I came around the corner, I had two options—hit the middle of the pack going fifty miles per hour or lay the bike down and take my chances. I laid the bike down, and the result was a trip to the ER and a totaled motorcycle. As a result of laying the bike down, I jammed and broke my left big toe. I had never given much thought to my left big toe before that event. I can tell you that my left big toe had a large portion of my attention for many days after that. My toe hurt for weeks, and it was no fun putting on shoes. My toe is a part of my body. It plays a very important part; it enables me to walk. My left big toe may not get all the glamor bestowed on a heart or lungs, but if you break it, it will have your full attention! So it is in the body of Christ. Some of us might be the proverbial big toe in the ministry, but God made us the big toe for a reason, and we are important to the church.

Another thing to remember is that spiritual gifts are only effective when employed in the power of the Holy Spirit who granted them. Jesus was very clear to His disciples that they could do nothing without Him. It was only through their connection to Him that they were empowered to do the ministry. Jesus said, "I am the vine, ye are the branches: He that abideth in me, and I in him, the same bringeth forth much fruit: for without me ye can do nothing" (John 15:5). Spiritual fruitfulness is only possible when we are connected to Jesus. That connection begins with saving faith and continues as we walk in faith with Him daily. An effective follower of Christ is one who is connected to Jesus and exercises his or her spiritual gifts in the power of the Holy Spirit.

The Great Danger

There is a great danger when one becomes an effective follower of Christ; that danger is pride. It has been said that pride is the "supreme temptation from Satan because pride is at the heart of his own evil nature."[30] The Bible warns: "Every one that is proud in heart is an abomination to the Lord" (Prov. 16:5a). Pride is such an easy trap to fall into because it is at the root of all sin. Even after we are saved by faith in Jesus, our fallen flesh continues to resist all that is godly through pride and rebellion. Like Satan, our flesh desires to sit on the throne and thus make us our own god.

A simple scenario will serve to illustrate the danger of pride. Imagine for a moment that a follower of Christ begins to experience great success in service to the Lord. Suppose God is pleased to use a pastor in a mighty way, and many souls are won to Christ through his proclaiming of the gospel. The church where this pastor serves experiences impressive numerical growth, and soon many are asking him how he does it. The trap is subtle, but it is there nonetheless. In asking how the pastor does it, the well-intentioned people have credited the pastor with the flourishing ministry. They have credited the pastor with doing something God did. The temptation for the pastor would be to agree with the accolades and praise of the people. The temptation would be to embrace some celebrity status and take on an unspoken attitude of being better than some other pastor whose church is barely growing at all. The trap is all too real and is played out every day in similar scenarios in the lives of our Lord's followers. Pride is perhaps Satan's greatest trap, and how easily we are persuaded to step into it!

The Bible warns us that God is against the proud. James 4:6b tells us: "God resisteth the proud." The Greek word for "resisteth" is the word

---

[30] John MacArthur, *Daniel: God's Control over Rulers and Nations*, MacArthur Bible Studies (Nashville, TN: W Publishing, 2000), 45.

antitasso. It is a compound word made up of the prefix *anti* and the root word *tasso*. The prefix *anti* means the opposite of whatever the root word means. The word *tasso* means to put in order or array. Therefore, the word *antitasso* means to put in disarray or to put out of order. God will cause the proud to be put in disarray; the plans of the proud will be brought to confusion and disorder.[31] We can never be an effective follower of Christ when we have pride in our hearts. God will never share His glory with a man or a ministry. The effective follower of Christ must be careful to guard against pride when God is pleased to use one of His own for His glory.

Humility is the opposite of pride. Humility is about having a servant's heart—a willingness to set aside self for the benefit of others. Being an effective follower of Jesus is not about self-exaltation, the applause of man, or the accolades of those watching. It's not about attaining some celebrity status or upper position in the church. Humility is ever pointing people to Jesus, even when He is pleased to use us in some notable way. A great biblical example of this truth is seen in John the Baptist. Some of John's disciples came to him and reported that Jesus's ministry was booming; they said, "and all men come to him" (John 3:26b). John's reply was one for the ages. Rather than be offended at Jesus's success, John simply said, "He must increase, but I must decrease" (John 3:30). May we have the same mind as John the Baptist. In every aspect of our Christian ministry and service to our Lord, may He increase and we decrease.

Summary

We have defined the effective follower of Christ as one who is living a habitually surrendered life to the power of the Holy Spirit whereby the Holy Spirit produces good works, which bring honor and glory to God the Father. Each follower of Christ is endowed by the Holy Spirit with spiritual gifts unique to who God created that person to be. Effectiveness in the Christian life begins with God's saving work in our lives and is followed by our faithful diligence to add to our faith the spiritual elements that enhance our ability to effectively serve. To our saving faith we are to add

---

[31] Junior Hill, *Big Shots and Little Squirts* (Hartselle, AL: JHI Publishers, 2008), 20.

virtue, knowledge, temperance, patience, godliness, brotherly kindness, and charity or love (2 Pet. 1:5–8).

God's equipping of His followers to serve effectively must be coupled with the follower's willingness to be a servant. The effective follower of Christ is willing to surrender all to the Lord. Jesus is the master of our bodies, our minds, our strength, our resources, and our time. The redeemed of Christ owe all to Him. We must be willing to serve in the time and place of God's choosing. The effective follower of Christ does not serve for personal gain or glory but rather is willing to simply do the Master's bidding. John the Baptist said it best when asked about the success of his ministry as compared to that of Christ: "He must increase, but I must decrease" (John 3:30).

All effective ministry is carried out in the power of the Holy Spirit. The flesh can produce no works that are of value for the kingdom of Christ. A follower of Christ may possess many wonderful spiritual gifts; however, the follower of Christ who is surrendered to the power of the Holy Spirit becomes a mighty instrument in the hand of God. Our talents, abilities, and spiritual gifts are only effective when directed and empowered by God.

Finally, every follower of Christ must be on guard against the ever-present temptation to pride. The Bible warns that pride brings three things that are contrary to the work of the Spirit. First, with pride comes shame. Proverbs 11:2a says, "When pride cometh, then cometh shame." Those who boast in their hearts will soon discover they are not as big and powerful as they perceived. Second, with pride comes contentions. Proverbs 13:10a says, "Only by pride cometh contention." God is not the author of confusion or disunity. Pride is most often the culprit when God's people fight and act unlovingly toward one another. Third, pride comes before a fall. Proverbs 16:18 warns, "Pride goeth before destruction, and an haughty spirit before a fall." The follower of Christ who is effective will only continue to be effective to the degree pride is resisted and the heart is kept humble before God. Remember, God shares His glory with no man, no matter how spiritual or successful in the ministry that person may seem to be. Humility in the ministry is one of the very first litmus tests that should be examined to see if what is happening is of God. May we all beware of the destructive effect of pride.

Five
COURAGE

O n July 29, 1967, the USS Forrestal, the navy's premier aircraft carrier at the time, was operating in the Gulf of Tonkin off the coast of Vietnam. The flight deck was full of aircraft, loaded with fuel and live ordinance, preparing for a launch and mission as part of the Vietnam War. While preparations were under way for the launch, a rocket was accidentally fired from one of the F-4 Phantom aircraft on the fantail of the flight deck. The rocket screamed across the deck and struck an A-4 aircraft on the starboard side of the ship. The ensuing explosion and fireball soon engulfed many of the aircraft parked on the fantail. Each of these aircraft were fully fueled, and most of them were loaded with live bombs and rockets. The aft end of the flight deck was instantly turned into a flaming inferno with live ordinance that would begin cooking off at any time.

Amid all the chaos caused by the explosion and the fire, a one-thousand-pound bomb from one of the aircraft had fallen onto the flight deck. Chief Aviation Boatswain's Mate Gerald Farrier saw the bomb on the deck, grabbed a small fire extinguisher, and ran into the flames toward the bomb in an attempt to drive the fire away from the bomb and prevent it from detonating. Chief Farrier was too late. Just as he arrived at the bomb, it exploded. The blast killed the chief instantly, and the fragments from the bomb case killed most of the first response fire team who were already on scene fighting the fire. In total, some 134 brave sailors would lose their lives that day with some 161 more sailors injured.

What would cause a man to pick up a small fire extinguisher and run into a fire toward a one-thousand-pound bomb? The word we are looking for here is courage. Courage is defined in various ways, often depending on the context in which it is used. However, the overarching definition centers around the ability to "do something that frightens" us or to persevere in action where we know there is danger.[32] Courage is not the absence of fear but rather the determination to act despite the fear. The chief knew all about the danger and what might happen when he grabbed the fire extinguisher and ran into the fire. His courage drove him to act in the best interest of others, regardless of the danger.

To be a follower of Christ requires courage. The Bible tells us that we are engaged in spiritual warfare every day. The apostle Paul reminded us: "For we wrestle not against flesh and blood, but against principalities, against powers, against the rulers of the darkness of this world, against spiritual wickedness in high places" (Eph. 6:12). When a genuine follower of Christ is growing in faith and being used of God for His glory and the growth of His kingdom on earth, the forces of hell will certainly stand against that follower of Christ. The battle is always the hottest when we stand on the front line. It takes spiritual courage to stand in the trenches where we know there is danger. It takes spiritual courage to stand for Christ when we know it will cost us pain, suffering, and even lose in this life. We find an example of what spiritual courage looks like among the followers of Christ when we examine the lives of three young Hebrew men who were captive in Babylon.

Courageous Young Men

In Daniel 3 we find the story of three Hebrew men who were taken captive by the Babylonian king—Nebuchadnezzar. These men were placed in what we might call a Babylonian university and taught all the ways of the Chaldeans for three years. Their Hebrew names—Hananiah, Mishael, and Azariah—were changed to Babylonian names—Shadrach, Meshach, and Abed-nego. These men were placed under the most extensive efforts imaginable to change their worldview and cause doubt about all they had ever known or believed. They were taught about the Babylonian gods, placed under the influence of pagan Babylonian society, and pressured on

---

[32] Catherine Soanes and Angus Stevenson, eds., *Concise Oxford English Dictionary* (Oxford: Oxford University Press, 2004).

every side to forsake all they had ever believed about the true and living God—Jehovah God of Israel. Yet we find these men were courageous followers of their God. They learned all they were expected to learn without compromising their devotion to the true and living God.

As we read the story surrounding these three Hebrew men, we discover there came a day when Nebuchadnezzar decided to impose a single state religion upon the nation of Babylon. Daniel 3 tells us how Nebuchadnezzar built an image—a statue—on the plain of Dura. This statue was ninety feet tall and covered in gold. Nebuchadnezzar decreed that all the leaders of his nation would gather on the plain of Dura and worship this image as a sign of their devotion and commitment to him and the nation. Hananiah, Mishael, and Azariah were serving as leaders in the nation of Babylon. The command to worship this image was a crisis point for these three courageous followers of God. They knew God's law forbad them from worshipping anyone or anything but God. The first of the ten commandments states, "Thou shalt have no other gods before me" (Exod. 20:3). The second commandment states, "Thou shalt not make unto thee any graven image" (Exod. 20:4). These men were immediately placed on the horns of a dilemma. They had to choose between obeying Nebuchadnezzar or obeying God. The penalty for disobeying Nebuchadnezzar was death by being burned alive in a fiery furnace.

When the time came for the leaders of Babylon to bow before this image on the plain of Dura, the three Hebrew boys refused. Their refusal to bow before the image took incredible courage. They knew full well that king Nebuchadnezzar would follow through with his threat, and they would be burned alive. Yet they courageously chose to obey God and leave the consequences in His hands.

The Bible tells us that Nebuchadnezzar was furious when he was informed of the refusal of Hananiah, Mishael, and Azariah to worship the image. The king called the three men before him and offered them one last chance to worship the image. Their response to the king's offer is renowned among the courageous followers of Christ. "Shadrach, Meshach, and Abed-nego, answered and said to the king, O Nebuchadnezzar, we are not careful to answer thee in this matter. If it be so, our God whom we serve is able to deliver us from the burning fiery furnace, and he will deliver us out of thine hand, O king. But if not, be it known unto thee, O king, that we will not serve thy gods, nor worship the golden image which thou hast set up" (Dan. 3:16–18). This answer contains three important parts. First, "we are not careful to answer thee in this matter" (Dan. 3:16b). In other words, the charges are true; we did not worship the image when the command was given. However, the emphasis here is on the king's offer of escape if they would but reconsider and worship the image. The unanimous answer of these three courageous men was that there is no need for deliberation or consideration; worshipping the image is untenable, and we will not do it. They told the king they were resolute in their conviction and commitment to serve Jehovah God alone. Second, these men responded, "our God whom we serve is able to deliver us" (Dan. 3:17b). Expressed here is an unwavering confidence that God is fully capable of delivering them from physical death in the fiery furnace. They confess there is no assurance that God will choose to intervene in such a way, but that did not diminish their confidence that He was and is able. Third, they were resolute that one way or the other, they would be delivered from the king's hand that day. If God allowed them to die a martyr's death, they would be in paradise with Him very soon. If God sovereignly chose to intervene on their behalf and deliver them from physical death at that time, then all would know the true and living God of heaven overrules the affairs of man—even the commands of the mighty Nebuchadnezzar of Babylon. Concerning these three men, Matthew Henry has eloquently observed, "We have here such an instance of fortitude and magnanimity as is scarcely to be paralleled."[33] These men were the epitome of courageous followers of God.

The rest of the narrative in Daniel 3 reveals that God chose to display His power by delivering these men from physical death on that day. Nebuchadnezzar was good to his word; he had the furnace heated seven times hotter than usual. Hananiah, Mishael, and Azariah were securely bound and thrown into the furnace. Nebuchadnezzar sat at some vantage point whereby he could look into the furnace and watch the prisoners die. However, on this day, they did not die. Nebuchadnezzar saw four people walking around in the furnace, and they were not hurt; the fire had no power over them. The king said, "Lo, I see four men loose, walking in the midst of the fire, and they have no hurt; and the form of the fourth is like

---

[33] Matthew Henry, *Matthew Henry's Commentary on the Whole Bible: Complete and Unabridged in One Volume* (Peabody: Hendrickson, 1994), 1434.

the Son of God" (Dan. 3:25b). Nebuchadnezzar's comment concerning the fourth person was simply an acknowledgement of divine intervention. It is very likely that the fourth person was the preincarnate Christ, protecting these courageous followers in their hour of greatest need. The three Hebrew youths had honored God with their faithful allegiance, and God in turn had honored them by delivering them from the fiery furnace.

It has been said that, "A man really believes not what he recites in his creed, but only the things he is ready to die for."[34] Hananiah, Mishael, and Azariah were living examples of that truth. They were willing to die for the God they believed in. The courage of these three young men can be examined and applied to the contemporary Christian life in four ways. First, there is a settled disposition; second, there is courage in the face of peer pressure; third, there is courage in the face of temptation, and, fourth, there is courage in the face of fear.

A Settled Disposition

The decision to stand for God is made long before a crisis event challenges us to compromise. The courageous follower of Christ lives in a settled disposition of obedience as a normal way of life. Faithfulness to God is effective during the storm because it has been the normal way of life when there was no storm. There was a pattern of courage and obedience in the lives of these three young men that enabled them in the moment of decision. The rejection of idolatry was as normal to them as breathing; it was a daily pattern of their lives. They had what we might call spiritual muscle memory where their natural response was obedience to God's Word.

As previously noted, the Bible warns that if we live for Jesus there will be persecution: "Yea, and all that will live godly in Christ Jesus shall suffer persecution" (1 Tim. 3:12). One of the underlying reasons most Christians today do not suffer persecution is the lack of godly living. That is not to say most Christians today live a sinful lifestyle; however, the sin of omission is just as serious as the sin of commission. Most Christians today, particularly

---

[34] Richard Wurmbrand, *Tortured for Christ.* (Battelsville, OK: Living Sacrifice Book, 1998), 62.

in the Western culture of material affluence, never share the gospel with lost people around them. They do not share the gospel for various reasons, chief of which is a fear of rejection and reprisal. The Bible is clear; if we are the ambassadors God has called us to be and we live a life separate from the sinful habits of a lost world, we will suffer persecution. The time to decide if we will stand for Jesus is now, before the crisis event. The time to establish a life habit of obedience and courage is now, before the challenges, trials, and persecutions come. We need a settled disposition, by the power of the Holy Spirit, that we will be courageous followers of Christ, even to the point of surrendering our physical lives if necessary.

How wonderful it would be for followers of Christ today to have the same kind of spiritual muscle memory—the immediate resolve to obey God's Word—as these three Hebrew boys had. How influential it would be if the world saw us as unwavering in our commitment to God. According to the apostle Paul this kind of settled disposition for Jesus is possible in the Christian life if we live in the process of renewing our minds. Paul said, "I beseech you therefore, brethren, by the mercies of God, that ye present your bodies a living sacrifice, holy, acceptable unto God, which is your reasonable service. And be not conformed to this world: but be ye transformed by the renewing of your mind, that ye may prove what is that good, and acceptable, and perfect, will of God" (Rom. 12:1–2). To renew means to make something new or different. The follower of Christ needs a new way of thinking—a new way of looking at the world. The renewing of one's mind comes by reading and studying God's Word. As we understand God's Word and the Holy Spirit applies it to our hearts, our natural responses to life's circumstances begin to align with God's Word more and more. Obedience to God's Word will become the habit of our lives, and disobedience will become the exception in our lives.

Courage in the Face of Peer Pressure

Hananiah, Mishael, and Azariah undoubtedly faced tremendous peer pressure. We know from reading Daniel 2 that these three young men served in significant leadership roles in the kingdom of Babylon. They had been elevated to places of leadership as the close companions of Daniel. There is little doubt that their friends, peers in government service, and even acquaintances encouraged them to conform to the king's demand to bow before the image. We can easily imagine the lines of argument and attempted persuasion. Some would have reasoned, "You can bow on the outside and yet maintain your integrity of heart on the inside. After all, the king cannot see that your heart is fully dedicated to the God of Israel." Perhaps others would have suggested, "You are far from Israel, so no one will know if you bow this one time. After all the public attention has subsided, worship whatever god you prefer." Still others would have suggested that it was no big deal to simply go with the flow. The suggestion would have been, "Just blend in and don't cause any ripples in the program."

These are the same peer pressures the follower of Christ experiences today. The world seeks to press us into its mold and conform us to its sinful image. In the same passage we just referenced, Paul said, "I beseech you therefore, brethren, by the mercies of God, that ye present your bodies a living sacrifice, holy, acceptable unto God, which is your reasonable service. And be not conformed to this world: but be ye transformed by the renewing of your mind, that ye may prove what is that good, and acceptable, and perfect, will of God" (Rom. 12:1–2). In view of God's mercy toward us, the apostle Paul is calling on followers of Christ to make a full surrender to Him. The idea of offering our bodies as a sacrifice to God has nothing to do with atonement; that was taken care of by the perfect sacrifice Jesus offered on the cross of Calvary. When the follower of Christ presents his or her body as a sacrifice to God, it is like a love offering because of what God has already done for us.

Then Paul warns against being forced into the world's mold; we are not to be conformed to this world. Secular society has a definitive worldview that is decidedly centered on the flesh. All that drives and motivates the world is self-centered and seeks to make humans the masters of their own world and destiny. We are not to be drawn into the world's way of thinking. It takes courage to walk against the crowd or swim against the current. The custom of our day says to do whatever your heart desires and enjoy the sinful pleasures of this world to the fullest. By contrast, God calls us to purity, holiness, and obedience to His Word. God's Word informs us that life is not all about the here and now; there is a day of accountability when this life is over. We have an obligation before God to live in a way that pleases and honors His holy name. It has often been said that any dead fish can float downstream with the current, but it takes a live fish to swim against the current and move upstream. May we be courageous followers of Christ and by the power of the Holy Spirit swim against the current of the wicked world in which we live. May we be courageous and stand against the peer pressure that comes upon us each day.

Courage in the Face of Temptation

Temptation can come to a person in many forms; however, one of the most powerful forms of temptation has to do with passions, or fleshly appetites. One writer said, "It is always difficult to put the appetites of the flesh in subjection. The devil knows this and often makes temptation really appeal to fleshly appetites."[35] One can only imagine the incredible temptation presented to the three Hebrew youths concerning the power, prestige, and high society lifestyle they enjoyed as upper government officials in the Babylonian empire. They were living the good life. These men were educated, enjoyed favor with the king, and were best friends with Daniel, the prime minister of the nation. They knew full well that if they did not bow to the image, compromise, and go along with the program of the king, they would lose it all. It took an uncommon courage to choose God over the pleasures, wealth, and success of this world.

There will come times in life when you and I will have to make the same kind of choice. Do we compromise our integrity for expediency—to be successful in this world—or do we stand firm in our conviction to honor God? One writer pointed out that temptation pressures us to yield to an action that is against our convictions—convictions we received from God.[36] None of us are immune to temptation, particularly the temptations that appeal to our passions. Satan knows just how to get at the weaknesses of our flesh. The apostle John set forth three sins that are endemic to all of humanity: "For all that is in the world, the lust of the flesh, and the lust of

---

[35] John Butler, *Daniel: The Man of Loyalty*, vol. 21, Bible Biography Series. (Clinton, IA: LBC Publications, 2007), 49.

[36] Martin Manser, *Dictionary of Bible Themes: The Accessible and Comprehensive Tool for Topical Studies* (London: Martin Manser, 2009), 6248.

the eyes, and the pride of life, is not of the Father, but is of the world" (1 John 2:16). The first area of sin, the lust of the flesh, includes far more than sexual sins. The lust of the flesh includes all worldly ambitions apart from the will and purpose of God. William Barclay summed it up nicely when he said, "To be subject to physical desire is to judge everything in this world by purely material standards. It is to live a life dominated by the senses."[37] It is natural for man to live by his senses. It is the supernatural power of God that enables a man to live beyond his senses according to the will of God.

The second area of sin that John warned of is the lust of the eyes. This is the sin of lust. It is inherent in our sin nature to always desire what we do not have. Even if we enjoy some level of material success in this world, it seems we are never satisfied or content with what we have. This temptation always connects perceived happiness in life with things of this world. We are tempted to look upon and lust after what we think will make life more fulfilling. This is a powerful deception used by Satan at every opportunity. The only one who can bring true and lasting satisfaction, peace, and joy to the human heart is Jesus Christ. Jesus is the only one who can fill the void that sin brings to the soul of man.

Finally, John warned us of the danger of the pride of life. This sin has to do with boastfulness. In our sinfulness, we are moved to seek the praise and adoration of others. We are so quick to boast of what we have done to gain the praise and approval of others. There is but one person we should seek to please, and that person is Jesus. As followers of Christ, we are called to serve Him in a way that brings all honor and glory to His worthy name. We should be like John the Baptist in seeking to see Jesus increased as we are decreased.

Hananiah, Mishael, and Azariah had all three of these things that men so often long for. They could have pursued the lust of the flesh; they had all the worldly success anyone could hope for. They could have pursued the lust of the eye; they were wealthy beyond what most people could ever expect and most likely could have acquired just about anything their hearts desired. They could have pursued the pride of life; they were government officials in the most powerful nation in the world. Yet, they forsook it all to obey God. May God grant us the same kind of commitment as we serve Him today.

---

[37] William Barclay, *The Letters of John and Jude*, 3rd ed., The New Daily Study Bible (Louisville, KY; London: Westminster John Knox Press, 2002), 64.

Courage in the Face of Fear

We can recall from our earlier definition that courage is not an absence of fear; it is the ability to do what is right or what needs to be done in the face of fear. We might, for a moment, imagine ourselves standing there with the three young Hebrew men. As we stand before Nebuchadnezzar we can see that he is angry. The king threatens that if we do not bow before the image, we will be thrown into a furnace and burned alive. The prospect of being burned alive is alarming, even in our imagination. For the three Hebrew servants of God, it was a very real threat. They knew the king would execute them immediately if they did not comply with his demand. We find here a case of courage in the face of fear.

The follower of Christ in our contemporary society must deal with the issue of fear as well. Perhaps we feel a tinge of fear and angst when a conversation turns to God or some societal issue for which the Bible gives clear and concise instruction. We are convicted immediately to speak up and share the truth. In that moment, the Holy Spirit reminds us that we are the ambassadors of Christ, and we have a message the lost world desperately needs to hear. Yet, there is fear because we know we will have to endure verbal and social attacks if we speak the truth, rebuke error, and share the gospel. There is fear that someone will ask a question or bring up an argument for which we do not have an answer. The truth is that the longer Jesus delays His coming and rapture of the church, the more persecution against the church will increase.

The persecution and martyrdom of God's saints was part of the first century church. Polycarp was the bishop (pastor) of the church in Smyrna. The Roman government put Polycarp on trial because of his faith and instructed him to deny Christ on pain of death. The Roman proconsul urged Polycarp to revile Christ and live. Polycarp responded, "Six and eighty years have I served Him, and He has done me nothing but good; and how could I revile Him, my Lord and Savior?"[38] Polycarp refused to deny Christ and at the age of eighty-six years old was burned at the stake. Christians continue to be martyred for their faith throughout the church age. By God's grace we may never experience a situation like Polycarp and

---

[38] Andrew Miller, *Miller's Church History* (Addison IL: Bible Truth Publishers, 1999), 167.

so many others throughout the church age have experienced. However, there will come times in the Christian life when we must be courageous in the face of fear.

Summary

The world is opposed God. Jesus said, "If the world hate you, ye know that it hated me before it hated you" (John 15:18). A true follower of Christ must be prepared for the attacks that will certainly come our way. To live godly in a wicked world will inevitably bring persecution and attacks. A godly lifestyle is a perpetual conviction upon the lost world that they need to repent of sin and trust Christ. Those who reject Jesus do not like to be reminded of their sin and true need of Him. Those who reject Jesus do not want to hear the truth; they don't want to see the truth, and they certainly don't want to be reminded of what happens when this life is over.

Like the three young Hebrew men in Babylon, a true follower of Christ is a stranger in a foreign land. This world is not our home. The moment we were saved by faith in Jesus, we became citizens of heaven. We live in enemy territory for now. We must exercise courage in the face of peer pressure. The world will do its best to force us into its sinful mold. It takes courage to choose godly obedience when everyone else is going with the sinful flow. We must then exercise courage in the face of temptation. The lust of the flesh, the lust of the eyes, and the pride of life are always tugging at our hearts and minds. Keeping our priorities in line with God's Word will help us stay focused on what is most important in life. Finally, we must be courageous in the face of fear. Fear can paralyze us. We need never be afraid to do the right thing. It is always right to do what is right. Even if God were to allow persecution to the point of physical death, He is faithful and will not allow us to be tempted or tried above what we are able to endure in His power (1 Cor. 10:13). Courage is not the absence of fear; it's just the ability to stay the course and do what is right despite the danger.

About the Author

The author is a church planter, pastor, Bible teacher, and professor. He has over 20 years of pastoral experience in the local church setting. He has a Doctor of Ministry (DMin) and a Doctor of Philosophy (Ph.D.) in Organizational Leadership with a major in Ecclesial Leadership.

Conclusion

Being a follower of Christ is more than simply taking up the title and attending a few church services. Involvement in a Christian denomination, an emotional religious experience, or membership in a local congregation will not make one a follower of Christ. A true follower of Christ begins with a new spiritual birth, which brings a renewed relationship with God. Jesus paid for man's sin debt on the cross, and it is only by faith in Him that our sin can be forgiven. At the moment of saving faith, we are born again spiritually and are the recipients of eternal life in Christ. There is no followership of Christ without first having a saving relationship with Him by grace through faith.

After we are saved by faith in Jesus, we must become willing apprentices. That means we must be willing to live life His way. Jesus called His disciples—His followers—to take up the cross and follow Him. Those who would be followers of Christ in this life must crucify self and allow Jesus to sit on the throne of our lives. There is no real followership of Christ if we do not allow Him to be Lord of our lives.

Also, the follower of Christ must be committed to spiritual growth. True spiritual growth takes place when we learn what God has revealed to us in His Word. The Bible is inspired—God breathed—and is the source of all we need to know concerning how to follow Christ. The Holy Spirit will enable us to do what we know to do from God's Word. Lazy Christians will be stunted in their spiritual growth and thus susceptible to carnality and failure in their Christian lives. We must be committed to spiritual growth every day.

Then there is the element of effective Christian living. An effective follower of Christ is one who brings honor and glory to God through an obedient life. Countless Christians sit in their local church assemblies every week, singing praise songs and listening to sermons. Sadly, many of them allow compromises in their lives that hinder their walk with the Lord. Most professing Christians today never share their faith with the lost world around them. How effective can a Christian claim to be as a follower of Christ if he or she never shares the gospel? After all, Jesus came to this earth to die on the cross for sinners. An effective follower of Christ will be a faithful ambassador of Christ while living a life that honors and glorifies Him.

Finally, a follower of Christ must be courageous. The secular humanistic society of our contemporary culture is absolutely opposed to God and all His church stands for. The world would have the follower of Christ make compromises to biblical truth for the sake of inclusiveness and harmony. While there is never a reason to be unloving or unkind, the follower of Christ is called to be courageous when it comes to standing for truth. Truth is always divisive; it calls for people to take a side. There are only two sides from which we can choose. We are either with Jesus or against Him. Whose side are you on? Are you a follower of Christ?

Bibliography

Alford, Henry. *Alford's Greek Testament: An Exegetical and Critical Commentary*. Grand Rapids, MI: Guardian Press, 1976.

Allen, David L. *Hebrews*. The New American Commentary. Nashville, TN: B&H Publishing, 2010.

Barclay, William. *The Letters of John and Jude*. 3rd ed. The New Daily Study Bible. Louisville, KY; London: Westminster John Knox Press, 2002.

———. *The Letters of James and Peter*. 3rd ed. The New Daily Study Bible. Louisville, KY; London: Westminster John Knox Press, 2003.

Bruce, F. F. *The Canon of Scripture*. Downers Grove, IL: InterVarsity Press, 1988.

Butler, John G. *Daniel: The Man of Loyalty*. Vol. 21. Bible Biography Series. Clinton, IA: LBC Publications, 2007.

Cairns, Alan. *Dictionary of Theological Terms*. Belfast; Greenville, SC: Ambassador Emerald International, 2002.

Cross, F. L., and Elizabeth A. Livingstone, eds. *The Oxford Dictionary of the Christian Church*. Oxford; New York: Oxford University Press, 2005.

Dulles, Avery. *Models of the Church*. New York: Image Books, 2002.

Elwell, Walter A. *Evangelical Dictionary of Biblical Theology*. Baker Reference Library. Grand Rapids, MI: Baker Book House, 1996.

Salmon, Marilyn J. *Preaching without Contempt: Overcoming Unintended Anti-Judaism*. Minneapolis, MN: Fortress Press, 2006.

Hendriksen, William. *New Testament Commentary: Matthew*. Grand Rapids, MI: Baker Books, 2002.

Henry, Carl. *God, Revelation, and Authority*. Wheaton, IL: Crossway Books, 1999.

Henry, Matthew. *Matthew Henry's Commentary on the Whole Bible: Complete and Unabridged in One Volume*. Peabody: Hendrickson, 1994.

MacArthur, John. *Daniel: God's Control over Rulers and Nations*. MacArthur Bible Studies. Nashville, TN: W Publishing, 2000.

———. *The MacArthur New Testament Commentary, Matthew 16–23*. Chicago, IL: Moody Press, 1988.

Manser, Martin H. *Dictionary of Bible Themes: The Accessible and Comprehensive Tool for Topical Studies*. London: Martin Manser, 2009.

Mathews, K. A., *Genesis 1–11:26*. Vol. 1A. The New American Commentary. Nashville TN: Broadman & Holman Publishers, 1996.

Miller, Andrew. *Miller's Church History*. Addison IL: Bible Truth Publishers, 1999.

Schaff, Philip, and David Schley Schaff. *History of the Christian Church*. New York: Charles Scribner's Sons, 1910.

Soanes, Catherine, and Angus Stevenson, eds. *Concise Oxford English Dictionary*. Oxford: Oxford University Press, 2004.

Spence-Jones, H. D. M., ed. *Hebrews*. The Pulpit Commentary. London; New York: Funk & Wagnalls, 1909.

Tidwell, Charles. *The Educational Ministry of a Church*. Nashville, TN: Broadman & Holman, 1996.

Utley, Robert James. *The Gospel according to Paul: Romans*. Vol. 5. Study Guide Commentary Series. Marshall, TX: Bible Lessons International, 1998.

———. *The Gospel according to Peter: Mark and I & II Peter*. Vol. 2. Study Guide Commentary Series. Marshall, Texas: Bible Lessons International, 2000.

———. *Paul's Letters to a Troubled Church: I and II Corinthians*. Vol. 6. Study Guide Commentary Series. Marshall, TX: Bible Lessons International, 2002.

Wiersbe, Warren W. *The Bible Exposition Commentary*. Wheaton, IL: Victor Books, 1996.

Printed in the United States
By Bookmasters